OVERVIEW

Overview

The world of work has undergone remarkable changes in the recent past. Mergers, offshoring, downsizing, and technology have all come together to effect enormous changes in what were once fairly predictable environments.

For example, do you remember when these things were common assumptions about the workplace? Working 9 to 5, operating by the book, and keeping your nose to the grindstone. A hierarchical chain of command was the norm, it was commonly believed that the company knows best, and there was a notion that once people were trained they were forever educated.

Well, times have changed and those assumptions are no longer true. Select each statement describing how work used to be to learn how it translates today. The whole notion of what a career is has changed. Having a career used to mean fitting into the ranks of a single profession, industry, or company and moving up one step at a time. The company decided when you were ready to move.

Nowadays, the traditional career path still exists, but the notion of what constitutes a career is more fluid and individualistic. The individual decides when it's time to move. And, as a last resort, the next step may even be a job hop to another company.

With all of this freedom, however, comes complications. You are responsible for making your own career choices, and it's not always clear which way offers the straightest path toward your goal.

For this reason, you need to take stock of where you are now and where you want to be. Then, establish a career plan. Your plan is your personal map that leads you through the confusing and often difficult decisions you need to make in order to achieve your career goals.

In this course, the process for creating your career plan will be explained. The first topic will cover how to take an inventory of your values, interests, skills, and lifestyle aspirations. The second topic will help you to identify your strengths and weaknesses. In the third topic, you'll pull it all together and develop a career plan that's based on your individual attributes and what you want to achieve in your career.

Think about your career up to this point. Have you drifted along like a passenger in a boat, going wherever the currents of life take you? Or have you taken intentional steps and been proactive about guiding the direction your career path takes?

Every so often, you should step back and give some serious thought about whether your career is on track. Are you heading in a direction you're happy with? Are you on a path that will help you reach your goals?

Managing Your Career

If the answer to either of these questions is "no," you should seriously explore your career options. In fact, exploring all potential options is an important part of staying on the right track with your career. So what are your options? Well, you can move up when you're on the right path. Or you can move over when the right path exists elsewhere in your company. Finally, you can move on when your company doesn't offer any path that will help you reach your goals.

This course discusses all the different options you have available when you're trying to get your career on the right track:

- First, you'll discover tips for making successful in-house job changes, as well as ways to make lateral moves in the same company.
- Then, you'll find out about approaches you can take to create and implement an effective promotion plan, and learn the best ways to ask for assignments that will move your career forward.
- Finally, you'll discover ways you can successfully move on to a different employer if you've exhausted all your options at your current place of work.
- In today's business environment, you can't sit back and hope for promotions to come your way with no effort on your part.

Keeping your career on track is your responsibility. If you know where you want to go, you can take the steps to make things happen.

Instead of being merely a passenger in a boat, you'll be its captain, navigating through your career to reach your destination.

Sorin Dumitrascu

It's performance appraisal time. Are you ready? Think back to the last time your work was judged. Were you clear on the purpose of the evaluation? Did you understand which standards you were being held to? Could you appreciate how the appraisal benefited both you and your employer?

If you answered "no" to any of these questions, you're not alone.

Performance appraisals are systematic reviews of your work and achievements during a defined period of time. They're done by comparing your productivity to a number of predefined performance measures – simple scales that answer the question "How well did I do at meeting this objective?"

People are often apprehensive of performance appraisals – and with good reason. It's not easy to listen to someone pronounce judgment on your hard work.

But evaluating work performance is one of the most essential aspects of the employer-employee relationship. Your performance appraisal can affect everything that is important to you at work – salary, career advancement, responsibility, and reputation.

As important as performance appraisals are, some people aren't prepared for them when the day arrives. They're unclear on the standards by which they're being judged, and even less aware of the criteria their employer is using to assess how they measure up to those standards.

They don't recognize that their appraisal is an opportunity to improve job performance, or to advance career goals. But you can use your employer's performance appraisal system to your advantage by concentrating on three areas. Select each area for more information.

Preparation

Preparation for your annual appraisal includes gathering evidence of your accomplishments and good performance, deciding what you'll say during your presentation, and developing the right attitude toward constructive criticism.

Presentation

Presentation during your appraisal maximizes your ability to get feedback from your employer, seek acknowledgement of your positive performance, and identify opportunities for improvement.

Planning

Planning sets a solid foundation for improvement through the periodic appraisal strategy – a series of performance checks that take place throughout the year and assist you in your progress toward your work objectives and career goals.

In this course, you'll learn about preparing for your annual performance appraisal. You'll also find out how to use this preparation to present yourself during your annual appraisal. And you'll explore how to use the periodic appraisal strategy to plan and document your progress throughout the year.

CHAPTER 1 - CREATING A PLAN

CHAPTER 1 - Creating a Plan
   SECTION 1 - Evaluating Your Current Situation
   SECTION 2 - Determining Your Strengths and Weaknesses
   SECTION 3 - Establishing Your Career Plan

SECTION 1 - EVALUATING YOUR CURRENT SITUATION

SECTION 1 - Evaluating Your Current Situation

When you evaluate your current situation to help determine whether you are in the right career, you begin by identifying your values, interests, skills, and lifestyle.

Your values define who you are and how you act in the world. Knowing what's important to you in terms of money, belonging, helping others, and self-development, for example, is critical. You can't be happy if your current situation doesn't align with your values.

To be fully productive and happy, you need to be interested in at least some of the elements of your work. Find out what engages you, and then evaluate your current situation to find out whether it contains those elements.

The appropriateness of a job hinges on whether it maximizes your skills. Evaluate what your strengths and weaknesses are.

Sorin Dumitrascu

Every decision that you make with respect to your current situation must be made in light of your desired lifestyle. Seek a balance between your work and home life.

THE APPROPRIATE JOB

The appropriate job

Are you in your ideal job? Is the career you've chosen the right one for you? Making this determination isn't easy – it takes a lot of self-reflection and analysis. Some people stick with unsatisfying jobs because it's so hard for them to dig deep and examine what they truly want from their careers. These folks are never really miserable, but they're never really happy either. You don't have to be one of them.

The ideal job isn't always about money or status, and it isn't always what you think of as your "dream job." Take Silda, for example. She had what she had always thought would be the perfect job. She was making a fantastic salary at a high-profile law firm in a big city. The job had prestige and provided all the money Silda would ever need. But something was missing – Silda was discontent much of the time.

One day, Silda was assigned to a pro bono case involving a low-income family and an unscrupulous landlord. In working with this family, Silda found her true calling – she loved helping people.

Later, after some difficult soul-searching, Silda quit her job and went to work for the public defender's office. She now helps low-income people work through the legal process. She earns much less money than before, but she's never been happier.

Like Silda, when you evaluate your current situation, you have to engage in some honest soul- searching. You'll have to answer some tough questions: Are you really happy doing what you're doing? Can you make changes that will allow you to be satisfied with your current job or should you search for a new position?

In this topic, you'll examine some factors you need to know about yourself to answer these questions. Factors include your values, interests, skills, and desired lifestyle. Taken together, all these factors can help you determine whether your current situation is right for you, or whether you need to make some changes.

As you go through this topic, make an inventory of your own values, interests, skills, and lifestyle aspirations. Your inventory will help you evaluate your own situation.

WHAT DO YOU VALUE?

What do you value?

What really matters to you? Money? Family? Status? Your core values – your principles, beliefs, and attitudes – reflect who you are and determine how you respond to events. They are also a big part of whether you are in the right job or not.

How do your values relate to your job? Well, if your job aligns with your core values, you're likely in the right job for you. However, if your job requires you to do things that go against your values, you won't be very happy. Consider two coworkers – Ree and Evan.

Ree and Evan both work in a high-pressure environment. Select both employees to learn more about how their values influence their enjoyment of their work.

Ree

Money and ambition are Ree's top two core values. She loves the challenge of a high-pressure environment – it provides her with the opportunity for rapid advancement and a big salary. Ree is very happy with her current situation.

Evan

Evan is miserable. Family is Evan's number one core value. The high-pressure environment and requirement to work overtime and weekends create conflict for him.

Although Evan likes his big salary, he'd be happier with regular working hours and weekends off. In fact, Evan is starting the process of evaluating his current situation to find out whether he can change it, or whether he needs to seek a new position.

Core values include money, family, self-development, belonging, autonomy, and ambition, to name just a few. People share many of the same values, but the mix of values and priorities is unique to each individual. You can determine which values are most important to you by asking yourself some key questions.

Money

How important to you is earning a great deal of money? Is it worth sacrificing other things, such as family time and friendships, for example?

Family

How important is it to spend time with your family? If necessary, are you willing to compromise on other things, such as money and a high-status job?

Self-development

Do you have a need to constantly learn new things and expand your mind?

Belonging

Do you tend to make the most of your friendships and relationships at work? Are you happiest in an organization that fosters a sense of community?

Autonomy

How important is the ability to work independently, without interference from supervisors or peers?

Ambition

Is it important that you are able to advance quickly in your career and earn the esteem of others?

Asking these questions is important. It can help you discover your core values and determine if you're in the right career. If you're not, it's easier to change early rather than wait until you're invested in a career path that doesn't really suit you.

WHAT ARE YOUR INTERESTS?

What are your interests?

In addition to identifying your values, evaluating your current situation requires you to get in touch with the activities that engage you and "ring your bell." In other words, what are your interests?

It's astonishing how many people work at jobs they're not very interested in. Yvette manages to get herself to work every day, but she has zero interest in her job. And while she's talented, Yvette's heart isn't in her work, so she doesn't perform well. Yvette's work won't sustain her over the long term.

Compare this to Daniel, who loves his work. He's fully engaged and motivated to do his best. He's also highly creative, and contributes good ideas to his organization. Daniel is very successful.

Question

Identifying your interests is easier than you might think. Hobbies, for example, can point you toward your interests.

What other things do you think can help you identify what you're interested in?

Options:
1. Activities you enjoy
2. Subjects you liked in school
3. Jobs that may intrigue you
4. Industries that might attract you
5. People you like
6. Movies that you've enjoyed watching

Answer

Activities you enjoy, subjects you liked in school, jobs that may intrigue you, and industries that might attract you are four ways to identify interests.

Many things can help you identify your interests, including activities, school subjects, jobs that seem intriguing, and industries that seem attractive.

Activities

What work and nonwork experiences have you had over the last few years that you really enjoyed? Were these experiences mostly adventure-related or intellectual? Do they all relate to the same interest? Do they correspond with what you now do for a living?

School subjects

What were your favorite subjects in school? Did you like math, art, science, or foreign languages? What extra-curricular activities did you enjoy most?

Jobs

Is there a specific job that attracts you? Maybe you'd like to be an interior decorator, web site designer, music teacher, or landscape gardener, for example.

Industries

Is there a specific industry that interests you? Maybe you'd like to investigate advertising, manufacturing, health care, electronics, teaching, or entertainment.

When you think about your interests, be careful not to confuse what you're interested in with what you're good at. The two aren't always the same. And don't worry if you don't have any burning or all-consuming interests. Few people do. Take the time you need to ruminate on what you enjoy, and then narrow it down to those things that truly engage you.

WHAT ARE YOU GOOD AT?

What are you good at?

In addition to values and interests, you need to identify your skills, and answer the question "What am I good at?" Skills are generally of two sorts: hard skills and soft skills.

Hard skills

Hard skills tend to be technical and specific to occupations. For example, being able to use a word processing program is a hard skill, and so is knowing how to drive a car, make a white sauce, and play a sport.

Soft skills

Soft skills are highly transferable. They're not occupation-specific. For example, being able to solve complex problems, keep an open mind, speak clearly and well, juggle several tasks at one time, and listen actively are all soft skills.

The questions that are useful for identifying your skills have to do with your capabilities. They encompass your ability to do a variety of tasks:

- organize work,
- coordinate the efforts of others,

- juggle several projects at once,
- solve problems, and
- communicate well.

There is another important question that can help you assess your strengths: Do you have areas of untapped potential? Many people have capabilities and strengths that they haven't fully developed yet.

For instance, Juan is good with young children and enjoys working with them. He may have the potential to be a fantastic teacher.

WHAT KIND OF LIFESTYLE DO YOU WANT?

What kind of lifestyle do you want?

So far, you have worked on identifying your values, interests, and skills. But these aren't the only factors you have to think about when evaluating your current situation. Before making any decisions about your situation, you have to account for your lifestyle needs.

Everyone needs food, clothing, and shelter, to name just the basics. Your ability to obtain the basics, as well as any extras that you may want, depends directly on the rewards you get from your work. So even if money isn't a high priority value for you, it's always an important consideration. Simply, you need to have enough money to meet your needs.

But money isn't everything. What about health insurance? Life and disability insurance? A pension? A severance package? All of these "extras" can make life bearable, and may be essential to you and your family. Many organizations provide some or all of these benefits in their compensation packages.

In addition to compensation and benefits, you need to think about other lifestyle issues, such as flexibility to schedule personal time, holidays, vacation time, travel requirements, and location.

Personal time

Do you have the flexibility you need to take time off for managing stress and meeting obligations, such as taking care of kids or elderly parents?

Holidays

Are you able to take important holidays off – Christmas, Kwanzaa, Ramadan, or Yom Kippur, for example?

Vacation time

Do you have sufficient vacation time to unwind and spend quality time with your family?

Travel requirements

How much travel does the job require? Will this cause a problem for family members? Are travel advances provided so that you don't have to travel using your own money?

Location

Are you in the location where you want to be? If the job requires relocating, are expenses covered? Will relocating adversely affect your family?

Above all, you should strive for a good balance between your work and home life, and seek a job that allows you to be flexible. Alternative working options like flextime, part-time employment, job sharing, and telecommuting are offered by many companies. These options give you more control of your time and your life. However, they sometimes come with trade-offs.

For instance, if you need to reduce your working hours to take care of family obligations, you may have to negotiate a reduced salary or take a job that has fewer responsibilities and lower status. If you decide to work from home, you run the risk of being cut off from important lines of communication.

Know what's important to you, what you want, and what you're willing to sacrifice to get it. Then decide how to create the optimal working situation for you.

Question

When evaluating your career, what are the questions you must ask yourself?

Options:

1. What do I value?
2. What are my interests?
3. What am I good at?
4. What kind of lifestyle do I want or have?
5. Who will mentor me?
6. What can I do to advance quickly?

Answer

Option 1: This option is correct. Knowing your values enables you to find a position that aligns with who you are.

Option 2: This option is correct. If you're interested in the elements of your job, you'll be much happier.

Option 3: This option is correct. Know your strengths and weaknesses. Your skill set determines what kind of work you're suitable for.

Option 4: This option is correct. Every decision you make with respect to your situation must be filtered through your lifestyle aspirations.

Option 5: This is an incorrect option. Finding out who will mentor you won't help to evaluate whether your current situation is suitable for you.

Option 6: This is an incorrect option. If ambition is one of your key values, learning how to advance quickly might apply to you. Otherwise, it won't help you evaluate your career.

SECTION 2 - DETERMINING YOUR STRENGTHS AND WEAKNESSES

SECTION 2 - Determining Your Strengths and Weaknesses

When you think about moving on in your career, you need to be able to capitalize on your strengths – those areas where your abilities and interests come together. If you don't already know where your strengths lie, you can use feedback from coworkers and your boss to learn about those areas. You can also use surveys to identify areas where you have both ability and interest. When you understand your strengths, you can work toward a more satisfying career that uses those strengths.

In addition to strengths, you must also know your weaknesses. If you don't, they will hold you back from meeting your career goals. Weaknesses are those areas of your job where you fail to meet minimum requirements. Sources of information about your weaknesses include your own self-evaluation, your coworkers, and your boss. When discussing weaknesses with your boss, be sure to prepare carefully for the conversation.

Sorin Dumitrascu

When you know your weaknesses, you can work to correct them. If the weaknesses are uncorrectable, you can learn to compensate for them.

IDENTIFY YOUR STRENGTHS

Identify your strengths

Do you know where your strengths lie? You should. Your strengths are like stair steps. When you consider moving on in your career, it's your strengths that will determine whether you're able to advance to a new job and, ultimately, whether you'll be satisfied with your work.

It's not enough to be good at things that you don't enjoy or be interested in things that you're not good at. You need to find those areas where your abilities and interests come together. These are your strengths. When your career makes the most of your strengths, many other elements of your life – job satisfaction, motivation, and fulfillment, for instance – fall into place.

Two employees use their strengths to find satisfying responsibilities. Vishruti and Telly both work for an insurance company – Vishruti as a supervisor in Quality Assurance, and Telly as a project manager in the Marketing Department. Both employees know their strengths and use them to seek out opportunities to enhance their careers.

Vishruti

Vishruti chairs the committee on process improvement. She is deeply satisfied with her work on this committee because it lets her combine her abilities in the area of quality assurance with her interest in working on a team with others.

Telly

Telly is on a temporary assignment working with the Actuarial Department. This lets him combine his project management abilities with his interest in mathematics. Because he's good at the job and enjoys it, he earns the recognition that he craves.

Most professionals know their strengths, and you may have a good idea of where yours lie. Informal feedback from coworkers and friends, as well as performance appraisals from supervisors, are two good sources of information.

You can also learn about your strengths by using a questionnaire or survey.

This example survey has a list of activities, along with columns for checking whether the activity is an interest or an ability. A checkmark in both the Interests column and the Abilities column for any activity indicates that the activity is a strength.

Is the list you made consistent with what you may have previously thought were your strengths?

One of the benefits of knowing your strengths is that you're better able to choose a career path that provides you with satisfaction and fulfillment.

Now, while your strengths are areas where your interests and abilities come together, it's generally your interests that will outweigh your strengths in determining what career you'll pursue. For example, Dan is good at math and financial analysis, but he'd be miserable as an accountant. His real passion is being outdoors and working to conserve animal habitat. Dan's interest is strong enough to drive him to pursue a career in conservation.

Question

Kyle has been working on identifying his strengths. Based on his survey, what are Kyle's strengths?

Kyle checked using tools, teamwork, mentoring and training others, and using technology as interests. He's checked using tools, leadership, showing initiative, mentoring and training others, and using technology as abilities.

Options:

1. Using tools
2. Teamwork
3. Leadership
4. Showing initiative
5. Mentoring and training others
6. Decision making
7. Using technology

Answer

Option 1: This option is correct. This is an ability and an interest, so it's a strength.

Option 2: This is an incorrect option. This is an interest but not an ability, so it's not a strength.

Option 3: This is an incorrect option. This is an ability but not an interest, so it isn't a strength.

Option 4: This option is incorrect. This is an ability but not an interest, so it isn't a strength.

Option 5: This option is correct. This is an interest and ability, so it's a strength.

Option 6: This is an incorrect option. This isn't a strength – it's not an interest nor an ability.

Option 7: This option is correct. This is a strength – it's an interest and an ability.

IDENTIFY YOUR WEAKNESSES

Identify your weaknesses

In addition to knowing your strengths, you need to be aware of your weaknesses. The benefit of knowing your weaknesses is that they won't suddenly show up to sabotage you and keep you from achieving your career goals.

So, what is a weakness? Specifically, a weakness is an area that doesn't meet the minimum requirements for a job.

For example, you may lack some of the training or education needed to do the job. Your technology expertise may be out of date. Or you may be unable to deal with the inevitable conflict in the workplace.

Lack training or education

When you're looking to change your job or advance in your career, you're likely to be in
competition with other people. Some of them will have better skills, more training, or a wider- ranging education than you do. Lack of training or education is correctable, so make sure you address this weakness.

Technology expertise out of date

It's important to stay current with technology used in your field and in your organization. It's also very difficult – technology changes all the time. The good news is that it's not difficult to find training sources for technology-based skills.

Unable to deal with conflict

Many people shy away from conflict. Perhaps they don't want to become angry and lose control in the workplace. Perhaps they're afraid of anger itself. If you're unable to deal with conflict, certain jobs and tasks will always be difficult for you, such as working with a team, working with the public, and even working directly for a boss.

Rather than allow weaknesses to hold you back, you must deal with them head-on. This is a two-step process. First, you must identify your weaknesses. Then, you change the ones you can.

To identify weaknesses, you collect information from three main sources: yourself, your coworkers, and your boss.

Yourself

You may already have a good idea of what you need to know, learn, and improve on. Look at your job description and assess how well you do each task. Review your last performance appraisal for comments about weaknesses or areas for improvement.

Coworkers

Coworkers have a different perspective than you do about your weaknesses or development needs. Ask a trusted coworker to give you some feedback on this.

Boss

The most helpful feedback on your areas of weakness may come from your boss. You can wait until your next performance appraisal to find out about these areas, or you can schedule a conversation with your boss now. Being proactive is usually better than waiting.

If you decide to meet with your boss to discuss your weaknesses, you need to prepare thoroughly for the meeting. First, schedule a time when the boss isn't stressed and allow enough time for the discussion – at least 30 minutes.

Next, during the discussion, keep some helpful guidelines in mind:

- State your reasons for the discussion. These should address your desire for self-improvement and include a statement of why you value your boss's insights into your performance.
- Clarify any statements by your boss that aren't perfectly clear to you. Ask for clarification on general statements, such as "You're not organized," and ask for examples.
- Don't get defensive. Listen to your boss's criticisms. If you disagree with anything that is said, you can follow up later, but don't react negatively.
- Acknowledge and summarize as you go along to be sure you understand.
- Close on a positive note by committing to improvement and thanking your boss for the input.

Kumar schedules an appointment with Linda, his boss, to talk about his weaknesses. He requests an appointment after lunch, before any of her afternoon appointments. He makes sure to request half an hour from her schedule. Follow along and think about how well Kumar follows the discussion guidelines.

Kumar: Thanks for meeting me, Linda. I want to talk to you about identifying areas of weakness that are holding me back. I respect your judgment, and I'd like to get your thoughts on where I can improve.
Kumar says

Linda: Thanks for the vote of confidence, Kumar. Actually, the only weakness I think you need to focus on is organizational skills. But we can talk more about this during your annual review.
Linda says

Kumar: Well, the review isn't scheduled for another three months, and I'd really like to start working on improvements now. Can you give me some examples of how I'm not well organized?
Kumar asks

Linda: Sure. Last week you had no idea where your team was on the serial integration project. And you've asked me three times for copies of the project standards.
Linda says sternly

Kumar: I've been working on two projects at the same time, which is why I've been a little forgetful lately.
Kumar says, defensively

Linda: That's not an acceptable response, Kumar. You asked for this meeting, remember?
Linda says brusquely

Kumar: I apologize. You're absolutely right. I need to focus on my organizational skills, and I can do that. Thanks for the feedback.
Kumar says

Linda: You're welcome. I'm impressed you're taking the initiative to improve your performance.

Linda says

Kumar made one mistake in his meeting with Linda – he lost his cool. While it's a natural instinct to want to defend yourself against criticism, you need to try to remain objective. And remember, the feedback the boss is giving you is precious, even if it's hard for you to hear. You need it if you are to overcome your weaknesses.

ADDRESS YOUR WEAKNESSES

Address your weaknesses

It isn't easy to accept information about your weaknesses, but you can't improve unless you know what they are. Once you've identified weaknesses, you can plan a course of action to correct them.

You can correct weaknesses in the areas of soft skills, such as written and verbal communication, delegation, and interpersonal skills, with classroom or online training courses. You can also ask coworkers to help by proofreading your reports or memos, if accuracy is a weakness.

And you can correct weaknesses in areas of hard skills, such as technical capabilities, with the same kinds of training as soft skills. In addition, the Web is a particularly useful source of information about the very latest technical skills.

Consider the way Clara takes swift action to address her weakness. Clara has a difficult time staying organized. Her boss suggested that poor time management might be the source of her weakness. Clara's company doesn't have an inhouse training facility, so Clara researches resources on the Web. She signs up for an online time management course that meets her needs.

By being aggressive in addressing her time management weakness, Clara was able to correct it relatively quickly. In fact, time management became one of Clara's salient strengths.

Question

Lila just received her annual performance appraisal. Her weaknesses were identified as presentation skills, accuracy, and interpersonal skills.

What can Lila do to deal with her weaknesses?

Options:

1. Ask her boss for suggestions on how she can improve
2. Take an online training course on presentation skills
3. Ask a coworker to proofread reports before submitting them
4. Attend a seminar on dealing with different personality types to improve interpersonal skills
5. Volunteer for assignments that will require her to make presentations to the entire company
6. Ask for opportunities to interact with customers

Answer

Option 1: This option is correct. Clara's boss is a source of information about weaknesses and how to address them.

Option 2: This option is correct. Enrolling in training classes is an effective way to address weaknesses.

Option 3: This option is correct. Requesting that a coworker proofread written documents is a good way to address accuracy problems such as spelling and grammar mistakes.

Option 4: This option is correct. Lila can improve her interpersonal skills by taking a course – especially one with roleplaying involved.

Option 5: This is an incorrect option. Lila needs to improve her presentation skills before she volunteers to do company-wide presentations. Otherwise, she's showcasing a weakness.

Option 6: This is an incorrect option. Lila needs to improve her interpersonal skills before she uses them on customers.

Question

Now you understand the importance of identifying both your strengths and your weaknesses.

Which are benefits of doing so?

Options:

1. When you understand your strengths, you can work toward a more satisfying career that uses those strengths

2. If you don't understand your weaknesses, they'll hold you back from achieving your career goals

3. If you don't understand your strengths, you can't be successful

4. If you understand your weaknesses, you'll be successful

Answer

Option 1: This option is correct. When an ability and an interest intersect, you have a strength. And when you're able to use your strengths, you're happier in your work.

Option 2: This option is correct. Weaknesses – defined as failure to meet minimum requirements of a job – can hold you back. If you know your weaknesses, you can work on correcting them.

Option 3: This is an incorrect option. You can be successful without understanding your strengths, but you probably won't be satisfied in your job.

Option 4: This is an incorrect option. To be successful, you need to correct your weaknesses – not just understand them.

SECTION 3 - ESTABLISHING YOUR CAREER PLAN

SECTION 3 - Establishing Your Career Plan

After you've evaluated your situation and you have a full inventory of your values, needs, strengths, and weaknesses, you need to pull it all together and develop your career plan. This can be done in three steps.

The first step is to develop a vision of the future. This is your long-term career goal. When you create your vision, be realistic and honest. Take into account your values, interests, strengths, and weaknesses. Then do some market research to determine where you should be in order to fulfill your vision.

After creating your vision, you need to determine how to get there, and develop an action plan. Figure out what knowledge and experience you need to acquire. Then figure out what resources are available for gaining this knowledge and experience.

Last, establish a time line for your development plan. Include the task of re-evaluating the plan itself. This will ensure you can keep your plan current as you and your environment change over time.

DEVELOP A VISION OF THE FUTURE

Develop a vision of the future

After you've evaluated your current situation and you have a full inventory of your values, needs, strengths, and weaknesses, you need to pull it all together and develop your career plan.

The career planning process involves three steps: first, create a vision of the future; second, develop an action plan; and third, create a time line for achieving your goals.

Have you ever had an interviewer or supervisor ask the time-honored question "So where do you see yourself in five years?" Did you have a good answer? Or were you paralyzed like a deer in the headlights?

If you don't have a ready answer to this question, you haven't created a vision for your future. Without a vision, you may end up bumping along in a dead-end job or a series of jobs that are ultimately disappointing.

If you have a vision though, you can aim for specific jobs and work responsibilities, which can act like stepping stones that will get you where you want to go.

Your vision becomes your overarching career goal – your guiding star. So when you create your vision, be sure to keep some important details in mind:

- Be true to yourself and keep in mind your values, interests, lifestyle aspirations, strengths and weaknesses, and your personal attributes.
- Don't get overly committed to a specific job or path. Your circumstances will change over time, and you'll change too as you live your life and experience new things.
- Don't get bogged down in details. Stay focused on larger goals and don't sweat the small stuff.

When you dreamed about your future, you may have asked yourself some questions to stimulate your thinking. Questions like these can help you define your vision: Is there a particular topic or activity that I enjoy? Is there a specific job that attracts me? Is there an industry I'd like to investigate?

Is there a particular topic or activity that I enjoy?

Not everyone can turn an interest into a career, but you won't have a satisfying career unless you pursue what you're interested in. Use your passions or things you enjoy to help form your vision.

Is there a specific job that attracts me?

If you always wanted to be a firefighter, a construction worker, or an actuary, now is the time to think seriously about becoming one. You don't want to look back in 20 years, regretting that you didn't pursue a job that you were really attracted to.

Is there an industry that I'd like to investigate?

You may be dreaming of joining an insurance company, or you're attracted to engineering firms or the aerospace industry. Think about what you have to offer, the kind of job you'd have, and the work you'd be doing.

It's a good idea to do some market research to make sure your dream job actually exists. And you want to find the industry or market where you can fulfill your vision most efficiently.

Begin with your current organization and think in broad terms about which areas might have a need for your skills. How might your strengths fit within those areas and what kinds of problems could you help the organization resolve?

Consider whether changes are coming along that might impact your vision. For instance, if you're interested in the health insurance industry, and if that industry is undergoing changes in how it conducts business, try to figure out how those changes might affect your vision of the future.

If you don't think you'd be able to fulfill your vision in your current market, research other markets. Use any and all resources for information. The Internet is particularly helpful. You may also have or want to get started building a network of contacts with whom you can share career information.

Question

Lauren currently works as a claims adjuster for an insurance company. Her very strong skills in mathematics helped her get her job, but Lauren doesn't plan to remain a claims adjuster for long.

Lauren is very ambitious and driven. Wealth and status are important to her. Lauren's strengths include leadership, administration, showing initiative, and decision making. She's weak in the areas of negotiating, using tools, and using technology.

Lauren does some research into her current situation. She learns that many positions are available in her own organization where her strengths could be put to good use.

Which vision of the future would make a good basis for Lauren's career plan?

Options:

1. In a few years, Lauren becomes an officer of the Finance Division of her company

2. Lauren takes a lateral transfer and becomes adept at setting insurance rates for groups of insureds

3. Lauren strikes out on her own and becomes the CEO of a high-tech company

Answer

Option 1: This is the correct option. Lauren's strong math abilities, her ambition, and her strengths could easily lead her in this direction.

Option 2: This is an incorrect option. Although Lauren would be using her math skills to set group rates, a lateral transfer isn't really in keeping with Lauren's ambition and values.

Option 3: This is an incorrect option. This vision would make sense if technology was one of Lauren's strengths. But it's not; technology is a weakness.

DETERMINE HOW TO FULFILL YOUR VISION

Determine how to fulfill your vision

Lauren has established her vision. She set an extremely far-reaching and ambitious goal. Now she needs to figure out how she'll fulfill her vision, and then develop an action plan for doing it.

How do you find your way to places you've never been before? With a map, of course. Well, when you travel your career path, you're continuously moving into new territory. To avoid known dangers, as well as to reach your destination safely, you need an action plan.

An action plan is a detailed outline of the goals and objectives you must meet in order to achieve your overall vision.

When you make your action plan, it's much easier to break the time frame into manageable chunks and work from the end point backwards. Nobody can plan 15 years into the future – there are too many variables to consider. But you can certainly plan for where you want to be a year from now.

In many respects, action planning is similar to the performance appraisal process. You figure out where you want to be or what you want to be doing a year from now to be on track with your career goal. Then you establish shorter-term goals and objectives that will get you there.

Why bother setting goals and objectives? If you don't do it, you'll lose track of your progress. You may even lose track of your vision. Goals and objectives enable you to check off the qualifications you need as you acquire them. You achieve a sense of progress that can sustain you over the long haul and motivate you to continue on your path.

Your short-term goals and objectives are established to correct deficiencies in your skill and knowledge levels.

Some deficiencies represent gaps in knowledge. For instance, do you need to learn about a particular subject area? Or learn your company's HR policies? The solution to knowledge deficiencies is training. Other deficiencies represent gaps in experience. Perhaps you need to learn interview skills or work on your ability to communicate with customers. You can only correct experience deficiencies with actual experience.

Training

It isn't difficult to find training resources. Many organizations have their own inhouse training facilities. Local colleges and universities offer classes in a wide variety of subject areas. The Internet is an excellent resource for locating training classes. The Internet is also a delivery vehicle for online training, which may meet your needs if traditional classroom training isn't available or convenient.

Experience

Gaining experience can be difficult. As many college grads lament, "How can I gain experience if nobody will hire me without experience?" Well, you can gain experience in other ways, such as volunteering, internships, temping, and job shadowing.

For instance, if you're drawn to humanitarian work, you can volunteer at a soup kitchen or a homeless shelter. This allows you to find out whether you really enjoy this kind of work. Or, if your dream job is selling investment products, find someone who'll let you shadow him for a day on the job. This will give you a good sense of what the job looks like "from the inside."

When you create an action plan, you need to identify the training and experience that will enable you to meet the requirements of your dream job.

For example, to become an officer in her company's Finance Division, Lauren will need to gain knowledge and get her MBA, Master of Business Administration. The degree is one of the qualifications for the job she wants.

Lauren must also identify the job experience that she'll need. For instance, she decides to look for an opportunity for a lateral transfer to the Finance Division. From there, she can study the environment and begin strategizing her path to the top job.

SET A TIME LINE FOR ACHIEVING GOALS

Set a time line for achieving goals

The third step in developing a career plan is to create a time line. This is something you can do at the same time you make your action plan. The time line is what sets an action plan apart from a simple to- do list. People respond to target dates; they don't like to exceed them. So assigning dates to actions helps to ensure the actions will be attended to in the desired time.

An action plan can take a number of different forms. The one that Lauren uses has spaces for her goals, objectives, and the actions she needs to take to meet her objectives. Beside each action is a date field. Lauren pencils in some rough dates, and later finalizes them as she prioritizes her actions and tightens the plan.

When she adds dates to her plan, Lauren is close to completing it, but there's one more task to do. She needs to make a provision for re-evaluating her plan on a periodic basis.

People change over time. The environment changes and priorities shift. Unless you revise your action plan to correspond with your personal changes, the plan ceases to be a useful tool and becomes a relic. To avoid this fate, you should include "Evaluate action plan" as an objective on the plan and give it an estimated time of completion.

Question

A year into Lauren's plan, her calendar program alerts her that it's time to re-evaluate. First, Lauren re-examines her vision. Has it changed? Not a bit. Then she reflects on her current situation. This has

changed quite a lot. Lauren's priorities have shifted; she's decided to start a family.

Which step do you think Lauren will take to address her new priority?

Options:

1. No action is needed
2. Lauren will suspend her plan
3. Lauren will adjust her actions and time line
4. Lauren will create a new plan that reflects her new top priority

Answer

Option 1: This is an incorrect option. While her vision has remained the same, Lauren's immediate priorities have changed. She needs to adjust her actions and time line.

Option 2: This is an incorrect option. Lauren doesn't intend to change her ultimate vision. She'll have to make changes to some actions – and especially her time line.

Option 3: This is the correct option. Lauren will need to adjust her actions and time line to accommodate the time she needs to start a family.

Option 4: This is an incorrect option. Lauren doesn't have to create a new plan; she merely needs to adjust her current plan to reflect her new priorities.

Lauren's vision hasn't changed. She still intends to become the head of the Finance Division. However, to accommodate her new priority, Lauren needs to make some realistic changes to her plan. She decides to give herself more time to achieve her vision.

For instance, rather than work full time and carry a full course load, as she does now, Lauren becomes a part-time student. It will take her longer to earn her MBA, but it will also give her time to enjoy her family.

By re-evaluating her plan and revising it to reflect her current situation, Lauren's plan remains a vital tool in helping her stay on the path to achieving her vision.

CHAPTER 2 - GETTING ON THE RIGHT TRACK

CHAPTER 2 - Getting on the Right Track
   SECTION 1 - Career Opportunities within Your Organization
   SECTION 2 - Making a Promotion Plan
   SECTION 3 - Seeking Out Assignments that Advance Your Career
   SECTION 4 - Changing Careers

SECTION 1 - CAREER OPPORTUNITIES WITHIN YOUR ORGANIZATION

SECTION 1 - Career Opportunities within Your Organization

No matter what your career goals, taking the time to explore your options is wise, since you can't rely on being handed a promotion. One of the best places to search for new job opportunities to advance your career is within your own organization.

You can seek a job change within your company in many ways, but the three most common strategies are identifying opportunities, seeking out professional development opportunities, and considering a lateral move.

SUCCESSFULLY MAKE AN IN-HOUSE JOB CHANGE

Successfully make an in-house job change

Setting your career on autopilot and letting it take you where it may is easy. But once you've reached your goals, it might be time to move past your comfort zone. Sooner or later, you'll probably decide it's time to go for a promotion or take on more responsibility.

Every now and then, you should take the time to explore your career options. In today's business climate, you probably can't expect an automatic promotion – you'll have to help the process along. One of the best places to search for new job opportunities to advance your career is within your own organization.

Changing jobs within your company

You can seek a job change within your company in many ways, but these are the three most common:
1. Identify opportunities
2. Seek out professional development opportunities
3. Consider a lateral move

IDENTIFY OPPORTUNITIES

Identify opportunities

The first strategy for a successful in-house job change is to identify opportunities and positions that may be available within your company.

Check internal postings

Most companies have a formal job posting program, which could be a physical bulletin board or a special online area.

Find out when new jobs are posted and be sure to check the listings on those days. And don't forget to check regularly – if you miss a day, you might miss a great opportunity.

Know company rules

You must be aware of your company's rules about the job change process – both formal and informal rules. Every organization has different rules. For instance, your company may require you to wait a year before you're allowed to apply for a new job.

Informal rules may exist as well. For example, some positions might be filled based on seniority or past experience in a different department.

Request information interviews

A great way to identify opportunities in your company is to request information interviews with people who would know what the position entails.

Suppose your coworker, Michael, holds the position you want. You could speak with him to find out what you would need in terms of skills and qualifications to do that job.

You've checked internal job postings, become familiar with the rules, and have interviewed several people for information about potential avenues you might explore. The next step is to use a visual representation – or map – of your company to chart out the possibilities.

Yvette is an administrative professional for a large cruise line. She really wants to move up in the company, and she's identified a few potential opportunities to explore. Yvette uses an organizational chart to map out the possibilities. She's interested in marketing and has been told she has many good ideas, so she highlights the Marketing and P.R. Department as a possibility. She's also taking night classes in accounting, so she highlights the Finance Department as well.

SEEK PROFESSIONAL DEVELOPMENT CHANCES

Seek professional development chances
Question
The next way you can change jobs within your company is to search out opportunities to enhance your professional skills.

Which do you think are examples of professional development opportunities?
Options:
1. Management training courses
2. Certification programs
3. Tuition assistance programs
4. Coworkers meeting after hours to discuss current projects
5. Health and wellness programs

Answer
Option 1: This option is correct. Some companies offer management training courses through their personnel departments. This is a great way to enhance your

professional skills if you're interested in a management position.

Option 2: This option is correct. Many companies help employees achieve certification in special skills. This can be a good way to gain the professional skills you need to obtain a promotion.

Option 3: This option is correct. Companies often assist employees with tuition costs for courses that relate to their jobs, or jobs they might want to apply for in the future.

Option 4: This option is incorrect. Many companies encourage coworkers to spend time together socially, and some even pay for events and social functions. However, coworkers meeting after hours to discuss current projects isn't an example of a professional development opportunity.

Option 5: This option is incorrect. Although a health and wellness program can help employees become healthier and improve their performance, it's not a way to enhance professional skills.

Seeking out professional development opportunities is the second strategy for making an in-house job change. This means taking advantage of any opportunities or resources that might increase your skill set.

Besides management training courses, certifications, and tuition assistance, your company might offer training in various software programs or leadership skills. Be sure to find out about all the different programs offered at your company, and take advantage of any that interest you.

Obviously, taking courses or classes will increase your skills. But pursuing these opportunities has other benefits as well:

- taking classes demonstrates an interest in developing yourself,
- taking classes shows you're interested in doing more than the minimum job requirements, and
- having invested in your development, the company will be more likely to want to recoup some of that cost by giving you more responsibility.

Since Yvette is already taking accounting classes at night, she checks into her company's tuition assistance program. It turns out she can be reimbursed for a portion of the cost if the skills can be applied to her work at the company. Her boss is impressed with her initiative, and notices that Yvette really wants to take on more responsibility. In fact, her boss tells her that when she finishes the course, she'll be in a great position to make a move to the Finance Department.

CONSIDER A LATERAL MOVE

Consider a lateral move

The final strategy for making an in-house job change is to consider a lateral move. Maybe you need a career path that plays to your strengths or satisfies your motivators. If this is the case, a lateral move – within your department or to another department – could be a good option for you.

You might even consider taking a demotion. You might think "But wouldn't that be career sabotage?" Well, not necessarily. Often, taking a demotion can put you in a better position to achieve your career goals by putting you on a path more aligned with your strengths and values.

You should also ask yourself a few questions. Knowing the answers to these can help you decide if a lateral move is indeed the best choice.

Why might a lateral move be a good choice for me?

Moving to a different job with the same employer in the same pay range can help you broaden your skills and experience.

This makes you a more valuable employee, potentially increasing your job security. It also leaves you more marketable, with more skills, if things don't work out with your current company.

Will a lateral move reflect negatively on me?

A lateral move can actually reflect positively on you if you use it to further your long-range plan and learn from your experience.

Moving to another department can give you new connections and show you how other parts of the business function, which are both benefits that may improve your career prospects.

How can I stay on the right track?

Before you make a lateral move, you need to consider whether doing so will put you on the wrong track in your company.

Observe the senior members of your organization. Have they obtained their seniority by spending years in one department? Or did they get there by gaining experience in many aspects of the company's functions? If the latter is the case, a lateral move probably won't keep you off the right track.

Once you have satisfactory answers to these questions, you can examine your motivations for considering a lateral move. In other words, what are the reasons behind your decision to take this path?

For instance, maybe you're taking classes to improve your marketability and need a less demanding position. Or maybe your family commitments require you to take a job with fewer travel demands.

Whatever your motivators, identifying them will make it much easier to successfully assess any opportunities that may come your way.

Before you consider a lateral move, keep in mind a few other important things – your company's internal employment policies, potential growth areas, and the chances of success and failure in your potential new job, for example.

Phyllis, a claims examiner, realized she wasn't on the right path to reach her goals. She analyzed health insurance claims and rarely met face-to-face with clients, which she loved doing. At first, she considered taking a demotion to an administrative position so she could work more with people. However, after asking herself a few questions, she realized this move wouldn't keep her career on the right track.

After considering her options and skills, Phyllis finally realized that a lateral move would make the most sense. It wouldn't affect her career negatively, and it would give her the chance to do what she really enjoys, which is working with people.

In the end, Phyllis made a lateral move to the sales office as a service representative. Now she's happier with her job and is in a better position to go for a promotion in the Sales Department.

Question

Harry is unhappy in his current job, but he enjoys the company he works for. He's ready to search for a new position in the same company.

Which strategies can Harry use to make a successful in-house job change?

Options:

1. Check his company's job postings for opportunities that match his skills and interests
2. Take advantage of his company's tuition assistance program to take a course related to the job he wants
3. Consider taking a different job within his current department
4. Keep tabs on his company's job postings by checking them once a month
5. Refuse to consider a lateral move because these moves always put employees on the slow track

Answer

Option 1: This option is correct. Most companies have a formal job-posting program, which could be a physical bulletin board or a special online area. This is a good place to identify opportunities.

Option 2: This option is correct. Seeking out professional development opportunities means taking advantage of any opportunities or resources that might increase your skill set.

Option 3: This option is correct. A lateral move is a good choice if you need a career path that plays to your strengths or satisfies your motivators.

Option 4: This option is incorrect. You should find out when new jobs are posted and be sure to check the listings on those days. Don't forget to check regularly – if you miss a day, you might miss a great opportunity.

Option 5: This option is incorrect. A lateral move won't necessarily put your career on the slow track. In fact, it can give you new connections and show you how other parts of the business function, which are both benefits that may improve your career prospects.

SECTION 2 - MAKING A PROMOTION PLAN

SECTION 2 - Making a Promotion Plan

If you hope to be promoted or take on more responsibility, it's up to you to create a plan for how you'll keep your career on track. This is known as your promotion plan.

Creating a promotion plan will benefit you in several ways. You'll achieve your goals more easily if you build your motivators into your plan. You'll have a better chance of achieving your goals when you ask for assignments that follow your plan. And having a promotion plan means you won't leave your career up to chance.

Creating and implementing a promotion plan typically involves four steps: choosing the role or position you want, finding out what's required to do that role, creating a development plan based on the identified skills you lack, and finally, when you're fully promotable, expressing your interest in the position to the right decision maker.

BENEFITS OF A PROMOTION PLAN

Benefits of a promotion plan

In today's business climate, most employees don't automatically progress along a specific career path. If you hope to be promoted or take on more responsibility in your company, it's up to you to create a plan for how you'll keep your career on track. This is known as your promotion plan.

Creating and implementing an effective promotion plan will benefit you in several ways:

- your career won't just be the result of chance happenings,
- your goals will be easier to achieve when you've built in your motivators, and
- you'll have a better chance of achieving your goals when you know which assignments to request.

Career won't be result of chance

When you have a promotion plan in place, your career won't just be the result of chance happenings. The direction it takes is up to you, and your efforts are the driving force behind your career path.

Goals will be easier to achieve

A key to success is motivation, and the chances of you being successful in your career depend on how motivated you really are. Your motivators could involve taking on new challenges, being able to take pride in your achievements, achieving future success, or reaching certain goals.

Better chance of achieving goals

With your promotion plan guiding your career decisions, you'll have a better chance of achieving your goals when you know which assignments to request. Instead of asking for assignments that might be easy or personally interesting, you can choose tasks that will help you on your path.

Consider Margo, for instance. For several years she has drifted along in her career as a sales representative, not really making any effort to be promoted. But then she realized she wants more out of her career – she hopes to take on more of a leadership role someday – and she creates a promotion plan.

Margo notices the benefits almost immediately. Since she knows which position she wants, she can choose the direction her career goes. She takes actions that will help her achieve that goal.

Margo is motivated to be a sales leader and starts asking for more responsibility. She takes on more clients and puts in the hard work necessary to stand out. It's not long before her boss notices her efforts, and Margo feels confident she'll get the promotion she wants.

Question

What are the benefits of having a promotion plan?

Options:

Managing Your Career

1. You'll achieve your goals more easily if you build your motivators into your promotion plan
2. You'll have a better chance of achieving your goals when you ask for assignments that follow your plan
3. Having a promotion plan means you won't leave your career up to chance
4. You'll be able to reach your desired income level if you have a promotion plan
5. You'll be in a better position to receive an automatic promotion

Answer

Option 1: This option is correct. Adding your motivators into your promotion plan will make achieving your goals easier, since the motivators give you added incentive.

Option 2: This option is correct. You'll have more success if you follow a plan that includes the application of both short-term and long-term goals. You should ask for assignments that will help you reach those goals.

Option 3: This option is correct. Your promotion plan keeps you focused on the actions you need to take to keep your career on the fast track.

Option 4: This option is incorrect. Promotion plans are effective for keeping your career on your desired path, but reaching a certain income level isn't guaranteed.

Option 5: This option is incorrect. In today's business environment, most employees don't automatically progress along a specific career path. If you hope to be promoted, it's up to you to create a plan for how you'll keep your career on track.

CREATING A PROMOTION PLAN

Creating a promotion plan

Now that you know the benefits of a promotion plan, it's time to actually create and implement one. Typically, this involves four steps. First, you choose the role or position you want to hold. Next, you find out what's required to do that role. Then you create a development plan based on the identified skills that you lack. Finally, once you're fully promotable, you express your interest in the position to the right decision maker.

Margo is a sales representative at a company that sells pharmaceutical supplies. She's working on the first step in creating a promotion plan – choosing the role or position she wants. Margo is determined to be promoted. She has decided to go for a job where she'd be in charge of a team of representatives.

Creating a promotion plan means identifying actions you can take to work toward a specific goal. The best way to establish your goal is by setting your sights on the position you want, as Margo has done.

The next step in creating a promotion plan is to find out what's required to do the role – you need to figure out what hard and soft skills you'll need. Since Margo wants a job where she's in charge of a team, she knows she'll need leadership skills. She also knows the position will require good communication skills, so she adds that to her list as well.

Question

What do you think are some ways Margo can find out what's required for the role or position she wants?

Options:

1. Speak to others who hold the position

2. Check job descriptions posted on the company intranet

3. Check the job description for the position she currently holds

4. Speak to people who are also interested in the position

Answer

Option 1: This option is correct. People who hold the position you want are good sources of information. They know what skills you need to work in that job.

Option 2: This option is correct. Job descriptions on your company's intranet will have complete details about what skills are required for the position.

Option 3: This option is incorrect. The job description for your current position won't give you any indication of what skills you'll need for the position you want. It can, however, help you prepare your resume, since you'll probably want to include the skills you already have.

Option 4: This option is incorrect. While other people who are also interested in the position might have some ideas about the skills that are required, they're probably as uncertain as you are.

Knowing what skills are required for the position is vital if you're going to go for it. But your skills are just one part of the whole package. To be promotable, you also need personal attributes that extend beyond your current position. These include things like good business sense, flexibility, political sensitivity, and loyalty.

Having these personal attributes, in addition to the skills required for the job, will help you be recognized as someone who's the "total package." Margo is doing a self-evaluation for her promotion plan and is listing the skills she thinks make her promotable, as well as those she needs to work on.

She's always relaxed when speaking to clients, and her clients and coworkers appreciate her willingness to listen. However, she sometimes has a hard time being assertive and taking charge. Margo has been with the company for over ten years, so she adds that to her list. She has a knack for finding different ways to get new clients, but she doesn't deal very well with change.

Question

The position Margo is interested in requires a person who has good communication and leadership skills. The person should also be flexible and loyal, and have good business sense. Based on what you've learned about Margo, which characteristics does she lack?

Options:
1. Communication skills
2. Leadership skills
3. Flexibility
4. Loyalty

5. Good business sense

Answer

Option 1: This option is incorrect. Margo is always relaxed when speaking to clients, and her clients and coworkers appreciate her willingness to listen. This means she has good communication skills.

Option 2: This option is correct. Because Margo sometimes has a hard time being assertive and taking charge, she needs to work on her leadership skills.

Option 3: This option is correct. Margo isn't great at dealing with change, which is key to being a flexible employee.

Option 4: This option is incorrect. Margo has been with her company for over ten years, which shows she's a loyal employee.

Option 5: This option is incorrect. Margo's knack for finding different ways to get new clients indicates that she has good business sense.

To find out what's required to assume the new role, you need to do as Margo did and draw up a list of the skills, qualifications, credentials, and experience required for the job you want. In other words, what will it take for you to become promotable?

Now that you know what's required to do the job, you can move on to the next step, which is to create a development plan based on the identified skills that you lack. The majority of your promotion plan should be comprised of actions you need to take to get the qualifications you're lacking.

So, if you've identified poor communication skills and a lack of expertise as your weak areas, those are the skills you'll need to work on.

Question

What are some ways you think Margo could acquire the skills she lacks?

Options:

1. Work with someone within her company who can help her figure out how to acquire the qualifications she needs
2. Get the training or experience she needs
3. Stay in her current job and hope she learns enough to be promoted to the position she wants
4. Watch an instructional DVD that explains and demonstrates the skills she lacks

Answer

Option 1: This option is correct. To acquire the skills you lack, work with a mentor in your company who can guide you in determining the best way to get those skills.

Option 2: This option is correct. The most direct way to acquire the skills you lack is to simply sign up for training or find some other way to get the experience you need.

Option 3: This option is incorrect. To acquire the skills she lacks, Margo has to take the initiative to get the training and experience she needs to be promoted.

Option 4: This option is incorrect. Although an instructional DVD might be helpful, the skills might not be taught to the same level Margo requires.

You'll recall that Margo determined she's lacking leadership skills and flexibility. To acquire these skills, she first speaks to her boss, who agrees to have her attend an upcoming course on leadership. Margo also hires a life coach, who teaches her strategies to be better able to adapt to change. She writes these actions into her promotion plan, and in six months, she acquires the skills she needs to be promoted.

Getting the qualifications you need might take anywhere from three to six months, or longer. But no matter how long it takes, continuing to work hard at your current job is imperative.

Your goal is to be seen as someone who's professional, reliable, and a hard worker, even if you don't plan on staying in your current position.

You've figured out which position you want, identified the skills you lack, and worked hard to acquire those skills. Now it's time to go for the promotion – you have to express your interest to the right decision maker.

Margo has finished her leadership training and feels better equipped to deal with change. Now she's ready to go for the promotion, so she submits her cover letter and updated resume to the Human Resources Department. In the meantime, she keeps a close eye on the job postings and openings that become available. Margo also maintains a good network of contacts in the company who can keep her in the loop on possible management changes.

Question

Margo finally gets a meeting with Edward, the head of the Sales Department and the person in charge of hiring and promotions. She hands him a copy of her resume, which consists of a list of all the positions she's ever held, and goes over it with him.

Do you think Margo did everything right during her meeting?

Options:
1. No

2. Yes

Answer

Margo's resume should have outlined all of her accomplishments, not just a list of her previous jobs. To get promoted, your resume should showcase your accomplishments, achievements, and skills. Margo did one thing correctly though – she gave a copy of her resume to the key decision maker and walked through it with him.

When you meet with the person who can make a decision about whether you'll be promoted, you should do two things to ensure a successful meeting:

- First, make sure your resume outlines all your accomplishments – it shouldn't be just a list of your previous jobs. To get promoted, your resume should showcase your accomplishments, achievements, and skills.
- You should also go over your resume with the decision maker, clarifying any unclear information and answering questions this person might have.

Question

Imagine that you've been working as a bank teller for a few years. You really want to further your career and decide to create a promotion plan.

Sequence the steps you should take to create and implement your plan.

Options:

A. Decide that you want to be promoted to office manager

B. Determine that you need office skills, management skills, and good people skills

C. Recognize that your office skills aren't up to date and make a plan to get the training you need

D. Watch for an open position, and then submit your resume and cover letter to the person in charge of hiring

Answer

Decide that you want to be promoted to office manager is ranked the first step. The first step in creating and implementing your promotion plan is to choose the role or position you want to hold.

Determine that you need office skills, management skills, and good people skills is ranked the second step. When you're creating and implementing your promotion plan, the second step is to find out what skills are required to perform in the role you've chosen.

Recognize that your office skills aren't up to date and make a plan to get the training you need is ranked the third step. The third step in creating and implementing your promotion plan is to create a development plan based on the identified skills you lack.

Watch for an open position, and then submit your resume and cover letter to the person in charge of hiring is ranked the fourth step. When you're fully promotable, the final step in creating and implementing your promotion plan is to express your interest in the position to the right decision maker.

SECTION 3 - SEEKING OUT ASSIGNMENTS THAT ADVANCE YOUR CAREER

SECTION 3 - Seeking Out Assignments that Advance Your Career

Asking for specific assignments can help further your career better than simply doing the work you're given. But unless your boss knows you want them, you might be passed over for these assignments.

When you decide you want to take on a new assignment, use three strategies to ask for it. First, ask at the right time. When you meet with your boss, focus on your accomplishments. And finally, you need to demonstrate your relative worth.

Using these strategies will help you be perceived as someone who has a plan and is willing to put in the work to go after what you want.

ASSIGNMENTS THAT ADVANCE YOUR CAREER

Assignments that advance your career

Jacob has worked at the same company for five years. He does whatever work his boss assigns him, and always turns it in on time. Chen has been working at the same company for just under three years. She goes out of her way to ask for assignments that are in line with the goals she's set for herself. Who do you think has a better chance at career advancement?

Chen has a better chance of advancing in her career than Jacob. Why? Well, asking for specific assignments can help further your career better than simply doing the work you're given.

Assignments can be skill-building exercises, opportunities to gain new experiences, or even a chance to show off skills your boss doesn't normally get to see. For instance, maybe you'd like your boss to notice how you've mastered a new type of software, so you ask for an assignment using that program.

The thing to remember is that you may be passed over for these assignments unless your boss knows you want them.

When you decide you want to take on a new assignment, you can't just march in and demand that your boss give you one. Instead, you should use certain strategies to ask for assignments:

- ask at the right time, such as immediately upon hearing about an assignment that fits your plan,
- focus on your accomplishments by emphasizing what you've achieved in the past, and
- demonstrate your relative worth by proving that you're worth more in the new assignment than in your current position.

ASKING FOR ASSIGNMENTS

Asking for assignments

A major part of getting what you want is asking at the right time, which is the first strategy for asking for assignments. As part of this strategy, you should consider several things – staying aware, avoiding bad timing, acting fast, and doing more.

Stay aware

Staying aware means keeping on top of developments that might lead to new assignments that fit your goals. Identify and ask for assignments before they're finalized by management. In the early stages, you may be able to influence the details of the assignment.

And be aware of any opportunities to provide something your company needs. If you can offer a new perspective on an old problem or find a way to do something more efficiently, chances are you'll get the assignment.

Avoid bad timing

Sometimes the timing is wrong to ask for an assignment. For instance, if you've just received a bad performance review that focused on your deficiencies, now isn't the time to ask. Resolve the problem first and then ask after you've made the necessary improvements.

Act fast

Acting fast means contacting the decision maker immediately if you hear of an assignment being considered that fits your plan. Express your interest and set up a meeting to talk about what you can bring to the assignment.

Do more

Doing more often makes the difference between being noticed and blending into the background. When you take the initiative to go above and beyond what's required, your boss will take notice.

Another way you can do more is by taking ownership. Being the person who actually deals with a problem when others have passed it off can result in a grateful customer praising you to your boss.

Question

You're a customer service representative and you've recently heard of a new team that's being considered for your department. You're interested in taking on the team leader position because it'll help you move toward your career goals. You set up a meeting with your boss, Karen.

What would be a good way to ask Karen about the position?

Options:

1. "I'm very interested in the new team. I'm wondering how far along you are in your plans for the team, including the team leader position. Maybe I could prepare orientation kits for the new team members."

2. "I'd really like to be part of this team. I know my last performance review wasn't perfect, but I think I'd make a great team leader."

3. "I'm really interested in this new team, and I'd like to be considered for the team leader position."

Answer

Option 1: This is the correct option. You're asking at the right time by inquiring whether the details of the assignment have been finalized and making your interest known by volunteering for an assignment that fits your career goals.

Option 2: This option is incorrect. Asking at the right time means making sure your timing is good. If you've just received a bad performance review, now isn't the time to ask.

Option 3: This option is incorrect. Although you're expressing your interest in the position, you haven't determined if you're asking at the right time. You should stay aware of assignments that might fit your goals, and identify and ask for assignments before management finalizes them.

You've scheduled your meeting to ask for the assignment at a good time. You should now focus on your accomplishments, which is the second strategy. Emphasize what you've done and relate those achievements to what you propose to do in the new assignment. This means selling yourself to your boss, perhaps by providing an updated resume. Your goal should be promoting yourself. Remember – being your company's most productive employee doesn't mean much if nobody in a position of authority knows about it.

Question

You've asked your boss, Karen, about the assignment. Now you want to show her that your contributions would be valuable to setting up the new team.

What do you think you'd say to focus on your accomplishments?

Options:

1. "I have the highest customer service ratings in the department and great interpersonal skills. They'll be even more important if I'm given the team leader position."

2. "As you've mentioned before in performance reviews, I have excellent people, organizational, and communication skills."

3. "Of all the people in the department, I'd say I'm the most qualified."

Answer

Option 1: This option is correct. You need to emphasize what you've done and sell yourself to your boss, demonstrating how the skills and achievements used in your current position relate to what you'd do in the new assignment.

Option 2: This option is incorrect. Focusing on your accomplishments means emphasizing your skills and achievements and relating them to the new assignment. People, organizational, and communication skills are desirable, but they're not accomplishments.

Option 3: This option is incorrect. You need to emphasize your achievements, which means selling yourself to your boss. Your goal should be to promote yourself.

The final strategy for successfully asking for an assignment is to demonstrate your relative worth. You complete the sale when you show the decision maker that you're more valuable doing the new assignment than doing your currently assigned work.

One way you can do this is to point out strengths that are underused in your current duties that'll come into play in the new assignment. For instance, you could volunteer for an important project that would showcase the skills needed for a new position.

But be careful not to sell yourself short in your current position. You have to make a strong case for where you are in case you don't get the assignment you're pursuing.

Question

You've asked Karen about the assignment and talked about your skills. But Karen is concerned that perhaps you're in the wrong position right now, since your skills are being underused.

What do you think you could say to Karen to demonstrate your relative worth?

Options:

1. "I believe I currently contribute at a high level, as you can see from my customer service ratings. But I have leadership and organizational skills that I could use as well if I'm involved in setting up the new team."

2. "Maybe I'm in the wrong position right now. I think my talents are being wasted. That's why it would be better if you'd put me in this new position."

3. "I don't think I'm in the wrong position. But I just have a feeling I'd be great in the new assignment."

Answer

Option 1: This option is correct. To demonstrate your relative worth, show that you'd be more valuable in the new assignment than any of your coworkers, without selling yourself short in your current position.

Option 2: This option is incorrect. You should be careful not to sell yourself short in your current position – you have to make a strong case for where you are in case you don't get the assignment you're pursuing.

Option 3: This option is incorrect. To demonstrate your relative worth, you need to point out strengths that are underused in your current position that will come into play in the new assignment.

Seeking out new assignments is a great way to advance your career. If you ask at the right time, focus on your accomplishments, and demonstrate your relative worth, you're more likely to be perceived as someone who has a plan and is willing to put in the work to go after what you want.

Question

Which are examples of strategies you can use to successfully ask for assignments that will advance your career?

Options:

1. Explain how you'll use your sales experience to generate more savings for the company if you're given a bigger sales territory

2. After receiving an unsatisfactory performance appraisal, you correct a few of the problems before asking for a new assignment

3. Describe how you've increased your department's productivity, and how you'd bring the same effort if you were to take on preparing all the reports for the department

4. Wait until you have all the details about an assignment before approaching your boss about the position

5. When you meet with your boss, describe the books you've read that qualify you for the new position
Answer

Option 1: This option is correct. One strategy for asking for an assignment is to demonstrate your relative worth by showing how you're more valuable in the new assignment than in your current position.

Option 2: This option is correct. Sometimes the timing is wrong to ask for an assignment, such as when you've just received a bad performance review that focused on your deficiencies.

Option 3: This option is correct. You need to emphasize what you've accomplished when you're asking for an assignment and relate those achievements to what you propose to do in the new assignment.

Option 4: This option is incorrect. When asking for an assignment, you have to ask at the right time. This means acting immediately if you hear of an assignment being considered that fits your plan.

Option 5: This option is incorrect. An effective way to ask for an assignment is to focus on your accomplishments. You need to emphasize what you've done – not the books you've read – and relate your achievements to what you propose to do in the new assignment.

SECTION 4 - CHANGING CAREERS

SECTION 4 - Changing Careers

It might be time to leave your current company if you can't reach your goals by staying there, and you've explored all avenues such as promotions or lateral moves.

If it's time to move on, you can use a few strategies to successfully leave your current job without burning bridges. You should conduct your job search while you still have a job, continue to do your best work until you leave, and be sure to leave on friendly terms.

By using these strategies, you'll be in a good position to successfully change jobs and keep your career on track.

IS IT TIME TO LEAVE?

Is it time to leave?

Your current company is great – you get along with your coworkers, your boss likes you, and you've built an impressive list of accomplishments over the years. So why would you want to leave?

Even if you like everything about your company, it might be time to leave. If you can't reach your goals by staying there, and you've explored all possible avenues such as promotions or lateral moves, you have to search elsewhere.

How to successfully change careers

If it's time to move on, you can use a few strategies to successfully leave your current job without burning bridges:

1. Conduct your job search while you still have a job
2. Continue to do your best work until you leave
3. Leave on friendly terms

HOW TO SUCCESSFULLY MOVE ON

How to successfully move on

The first strategy for successfully changing careers is to conduct your job search while you still have a job. This might seem counterproductive, but many employers are biased against candidates who are unemployed. However, don't search while you're actually at work!

Even though scheduling interviews around your work hours can be difficult, it's easier than explaining why you're currently unemployed. You can book interviews during your lunch break, or even take a day off and schedule several interviews.

Not only should you conduct your job search while you still have a job, you should continue to do your best work at that job until you leave. For one thing, finding your next position may take a while, and you want to continue building your accomplishments. Also, some managers feel betrayed when you want to leave their department. If you let your work slide, your manager might be more apt to deal with your poor performance – you may even lose your job before you're ready to leave.

There are a few more things to keep in mind for continuing to do your best work until you leave.

Add value

Continue to add value to your work as you search for a new position. You should continue to build on your accomplishments and add to your resume – the extra work you do this week could make all the difference in next week's interview.

Be aware of new opportunities

You may think there are no new opportunities left at your current employer, but you might be wrong. By continuing to do your best, a new position that meets your goals could come your way.

Think about references

Many companies have policies against giving references, but yours may not. Check with your employer – you should get a glowing report if you keep delivering quality work during your search.

Finally, when changing careers, you need to leave on friendly terms. This means avoiding burning any bridges on the way out. Even though it might feel good for a few moments to really tell off your manager, you could end up paying for it for years to come. Besides, it's just not professional. You should be positive and friendly to your boss and coworkers as you're leaving. Even if you've been miserable in your current position, leaving on a positive note will make your boss more likely to remember you positively.

Search while you still have a job

"When I was searching for a new job, I did all my research outside of work hours. I sent out resumes on Sunday nights, and made follow-up calls during my lunch hour, off-site. And I set up interviews for early mornings or after I was done work for the day. It wasn't easy, but I did it."

Continue to do your best work until you leave

"I made a point of continuing to meet all my deadlines while I was searching for a new job. I had to put in more hours, but it helped keep my spirits up. I still had a feeling of accomplishment at work. The best part was the glowing letter of recommendation I received from my boss!"

Leave on friendly terms

"When I left my company, I was really tempted to tell my boss all the things I didn't like about him. But then I remembered that it wouldn't get me anywhere. In fact, Frank, one of my coworkers, left our company but recently came back in a different position. I definitely wanted to keep my options open and leave on good terms."

Sometimes, the only way you can reach your career goals is to move on to a different company.

By conducting your job search while you still have a job, continuing to do your best until you leave, and leaving on friendly terms, you'll be in a good position to successfully change jobs and keep your career on track.

Question

Which are examples of ways you can successfully move on to a different employer?

Options:

1. You still complete your reports a day early even though you're searching for a new job

2. You believe your boss treated you unfairly, but you decide to put it behind you as you move on to your new job

Managing Your Career

3. You take Wednesday as a vacation day and schedule two interviews in the morning and two in the afternoon

4. You bring policy and procedure manuals from your old job to your new job because they might contain good suggestions

5. Even though you come down with the flu, you don't call in sick to work during your last week because you're afraid your boss will think you're faking it

Answer

Option 1: This option is correct. When you're searching for a new position, you should continue to do your best work at your current job until you leave.

Option 2: This option is correct. One thing you can do to successfully change careers is leave your current employer on friendly terms. This means avoiding burning any bridges on the way out.

Option 3: This option is correct. One strategy for successfully changing careers is conducting your job search while you still have a job. Even though it can be difficult to schedule interviews around your work hours, you should book interviews during your lunch break, or even take a day off and schedule several interviews.

Option 4: This option is incorrect. You should use the policy and procedure manuals issued by your new company to ensure you're following its guidelines.

Option 5: This option is incorrect. You should use your sick days as needed. You won't be able to do your best work if you go to the office while you're ill.

CHAPTER 3 - LEVERAGING THE PERFORMANCE APPRAISAL

CHAPTER 3 - Leveraging the Performance Appraisal
 SECTION 1 - Preparing for an Annual Performance Appraisal
 SECTION 2 - Making the Most of Your Annual Performance Appraisal
 SECTION 3 - Using the Periodic Appraisal Strategy

SECTION 1 - PREPARING FOR AN ANNUAL PERFORMANCE APPRAISAL

SECTION 1 - Preparing for an Annual Performance Appraisal

Preparation is the key to a successful annual performance appraisal. You'll need to gather evidence of good performance and accomplishments, prepare what you'll say about key issues, and look forward to receiving constructive criticism.

THE IMPORTANCE OF PERFORMANCE APPRAISAL

The importance of performance appraisal

Your annual performance appraisal is fast approaching. You're anxious about what your employer will find to criticize and worried that no one will notice your achievements over the past year. And will anyone realize that you're perfect for that new promotion? That's up to you.

The contents of your performance appraisal can help you support your actions, justify your career advancement, and prove your worth. But your employer can also use those contents to justify reassignment, discipline, or even dismissal.

Even old performance appraisals may have influence years later when you apply for a promotion, when you request a raise, or when you apply for a new job. These are the reasons to take every opportunity to prepare for what you're going to say and do in the appraisal.

Question

How much preparation do you put into your annual performance appraisal?

Options:
1. I get thoroughly prepared
2. I do some preparation
3. I prefer to wing it

Answer

Option 1: It's great that you get prepared for your performance appraisal, but don't make too many assumptions. At each appraisal, think about what you'll be evaluated on and be prepared to defend how you met your performance goals.

Option 2: It's good that you do some preparation, but it's important to be thoroughly prepared for a performance appraisal. You need to be able to present your accomplishments and to deal constructively with criticism.

Option 3: If you don't prepare for your performance appraisal, you're overlooking a valuable opportunity. Remember, performance appraisals are an important tool for keeping your career on the right track.

Your performance appraisal is a valuable opportunity for managing your career. Often, it's the only time in the year when you have your employer's complete and undivided attention. It's important to use your appraisal time wisely. This isn't the time for socializing or discussing ideas for system-wide improvements at work. It's about you and your career. Performance appraisals present a number of opportunities.

Performance

Measuring yourself against your appraisal's performance standards helps you understand your role.

Objective and fair standards provide a benchmark for you to appraise and assess your performance. They also help create a clear, shared understanding of performance expectations.

Planning

In a performance appraisal, you learn how well you're meeting expectations. You compare your employer's expectations with how well you're meeting them. This is an opportunity to develop a plan of action for setting goals and making improvements.

Potential

Promotions are often based upon performance. The performance appraisal is your chance to express what you want from your career and where you see yourself in the future. By speaking with your employer, you can also find out about training and development opportunities.

Some employees choose to look at performance appraisals like a dental exam – an uncomfortable meeting where the hard evidence of neglect is pointed out to them. Others may use appraisals as a chance to complain or criticize, or to vent about coworkers. But what these employees don't realize is that performance appraisal is about improvement, not blame.

Above all, it's important to your career that your performance appraisal be a positive experience for both you and your employer. A well-conducted review clears the air about the past and sets the agenda for a productive future.

Question

Which opportunities does your annual performance appraisal present?

Options:

1. It provides a forum for stating your goals and outlining your accomplishments

2. You learn how well you're meeting your employer's expectations

3. You can better understand your role at work by measuring yourself against performance standards

4. It's an opportunity to clear the air about problems you've had with coworkers

5. It's an excellent time to make suggestions about system-wide improvements for the workplace

Answer

Option 1: This is a correct option. Your performance appraisal is the ideal place for stating future goals and backing them up with your past accomplishments.

Option 2: This is a correct option. You can't meet expectations if you're not clear on what they are. You should never operate on assumptions.

Option 3: This is a correct option. The standards your organization uses to appraise performance are useful benchmarks for understanding work priorities.

Option 4: This is an incorrect option. Your performance appraisal isn't the time to vent about coworkers. Performance appraisal is about improvement, not blame.

Option 5: This is an incorrect option. Your performance appraisal is not the time to make general suggestions about the workplace. All suggestions should relate to you and your job.

PREPARING FOR A PERFORMANCE APPRAISAL

Preparing for a performance appraisal

It's an unfortunate fact that many employees go into their performance appraisal meetings without adequate preparation. Keep in mind that there's no upside to being unprepared. It's no fun to be blindsided by an issue you weren't expecting, or to fail to seize a golden opportunity in your appraisal.

Being unprepared to support your position or to advance your career goals means that you'll be forced into either a reactive or passive position rather than a productive one. Preparing for your performance appraisal allows you to focus on the key issue – performance improvement.

A number of activities will help you prepare for your performance appraisal:
- gathering evidence of good performance and accomplishments,
- preparing what you'll say about key issues, and

Managing Your Career

- looking forward to receiving constructive criticism.

GATHERING EVIDENCE

Gathering evidence

Before your appraisal meeting, gather evidence of good performance and accomplishments so you can support a positive position – the first preparation activity. Keep in mind that your annual performance appraisal is a judgment based on your performance over the year. But all human judgments are subjective to some degree.

By gathering evidence of good performance and accomplishments, you can support a positive position or counter a negative judgment. Make sure your evidence is clear, up to date, and relative to performance standards.

Evidence provides objective information about your success at meeting the requirements of your job. For example, are you in sales? If you've met your sales targets, have the facts and figures available to back up your claims.

It's also important to keep copies of your previous appraisals. This will help you show your success at achieving your goals and improving performance standards.

Ramesh is the assistant manager of the Admitting Department at a large urban hospital and is hoping to be promoted to manager within the next two years. Follow along as he discusses how he collects evidence of his performance and accomplishments to present at his performance appraisal.

Since I work with the public, one of my performance standards is "Communicate with a range of people on a range of matters."

This means the evidence I present in my performance appraisal should show what sort of information I've communicated, and to whom.

Throughout the year, I've maintained a summary of cases where communication was an issue. Where privacy was not an issue, I kept examples of reports, letters, and e-mails I've written, providing information, explanation, or response to complaints.

I also note how and when I gathered the evidence to show it's up to date and relevant to performance standards.

Question

Emelia works for a large graphic design firm. Her technical assessment on her last annual appraisal showed that she could improve her design software skills.

Which are examples of Emelia gathering evidence of good performance and accomplishments for her upcoming annual performance appraisal?

Options:

1. Emelia collects examples of the advertising campaigns she worked on throughout the year

2. Emelia keeps copies of her previous appraisals

3. Emelia highlights her performance goal of improving her design skills and makes a copy of the certificate she earned in her design software class

4. Emelia decides to show her creative skills by improvising her response to her appraiser's queries

5. Emelia prepares a career plan to show her employer at the appraisal

Answer

Option 1: This is a correct option. Emelia knows it's important to prepare for her appraisal by presenting her accomplishments.

Option 2: This is a correct option. Emelia can use her previous appraisals to show she met her goals and improved her performance relative to performance standards.

Option 3: This is a correct option. Emelia's course certificate is evidence of achieving her goal of improving her software skills.

Option 4: This is an incorrect option. Emelia needs evidence to support her accomplishments.

Option 5: This is an incorrect option. Although discussing career plans is important, it doesn't relate to Emelia gathering evidence of good performance and accomplishments.

PREPARING WHAT TO SAY

Preparing what to say

Although you will never be able to predict exactly how your annual performance appraisal will unfold, it will help to prepare what you'll say about key issues – the second of the three activities.

Before your appraisal, try to anticipate the types of issues you think will be addressed. Think about questions or comments that your employer may have, and think carefully about appropriate responses.

For example, did you face any barriers or issues that impacted your job performance? Be prepared to discuss how you handled those situations, and what you'd do differently to improve your performance in the future.

You should be prepared to discuss issues in a number of key areas during your appraisal:

- your job description,,
- accomplishments since your previous appraisal,
- the performance standards ratings,
- any areas for improvement or development,
- your goals for the future, and

- your self-assessment.

Follow along as Ramesh discusses how he prepares what he's going to say at his upcoming performance appraisal at the hospital.

| To get ready for my appraisal, I thought about what I want to accomplish. After all, my meeting is only going to be an hour, so I realized that I needed to do some preparation for what I'm going to say.

My supervisor is retiring in two years, and my career ambition is to take over as senior manager of the hospital's Admitting Department. I'll have some competition for the position, so I need to lay the groundwork now.

For example, over the past year, there have been several issues that arose when patient files were temporarily misplaced, resulting in a delay in admittance. I anticipate this will come up in the appraisal of my administrative skills, so I've made sure that I'm familiar with what happened, and I've come up with some procedural improvements for the system.

Of course I can't predict exactly what my employer is going to ask me, but I can anticipate the types of things that may come up. By preparing what I'm going to say, I can turn a negative into a positive. Instead of being blindsided by an issue, I'm going to use it to show my adaptability and administrative skills.

Question

Which are the best examples of Emelia preparing what she'll say about key issues that may arise during her upcoming performance appraisal at the graphic design firm?

Options:

Managing Your Career

1. Emelia prepares to discuss a problem that resulted in an important client leaving the company for a competitor
2. Emelia anticipates questions her employer might ask and plans model answers
3. Emelia prepares a career plan for her future at the firm
4. Emelia determines her supervisor will ask her about improving her technical skills, and she prepares
   to discuss the training course she's completed
5. Emelia makes sure she's dressed in a professional manner
6. Emelia ensures she has prepared extra copies of any documentation for her supervisor's file

Answer

Option 1: This is a correct option. Emelia should prepare to discuss how she handled problems and issues, and what she would do differently to improve her performance in the future.

Option 2: This is a correct option. Model answers will help Emelia to be prepared for questions that her employer might ask during the appraisal.

Option 3: This is a correct option. Emelia should prepare for the opportunity to relate her career plans to her performance appraisal and to discuss her goals for the future.

Option 4: This is a correct option. Emelia should prepare to discuss how she's worked toward her performance goals.

Option 5: This is an incorrect option. Dressing appropriately is important, but it's not part of planning what you'll say about key issues.

Option 6: This is an incorrect option. Making extra copies of documentation is part of gathering evidence, not part of planning what you'll say about key issues during the appraisal.

RECEIVING CRITICISM

Receiving criticism

Criticism is unpleasant, but it's also inevitable. One of the most important things you can gain from a performance appraisal is knowledge about where your performance is not meeting your employer's expectations.

Criticism in not necessarily a negative thing. In fact, you should look forward to receiving constructive criticism at your appraisal. In a way, criticism is a gift. It can help you understand how others perceive what you're doing.

It's important to resist the temptation to respond emotionally. By being prepared for criticism, you're more likely to respond in a positive and productive way.

Even if you anticipate some negative or unfair feedback, use the opportunity to find out why you're perceived in that light, and why your performance isn't meeting expectations.

Remember, when you're willing to acknowledge the validity of your employer's observations and performance ratings, it shows that you're serious about growing and developing in your position at work.

Constructive criticism opens up a number of opportunities for you during your performance appraisal:
you'll have a chance to demonstrate a dedicated and responsive attitude

you can show your employer that you're serious about performance, and

you can pinpoint opportunities to improve competencies and qualities that will make you promotable

Follow along as Ramesh discusses how he prepares to listen to criticism at his performance appraisal at the hospital.

In previous performance appraisals, I didn't always agree with my ratings. This year, I'm going to keep an open mind. I'm prepared to listen to what my employer has to say, and even if I disagree with it, I'll demonstrate a responsive attitude to his criticism.

Last year I got upset about one of my boss's comments. But responding emotionally just wasn't productive. This year I've prepared myself to discuss criticism in a calm and rational manner. This shows my boss that I'm serious about improving my performance.

I'm also prepared to use my appraisal as an opportunity. For instance, I know I could improve my organizational skills. If the opportunity arises during my appraisal, I'm going to suggest a mentorship with the chief hospital administrator.

Question

Anne has been working for two years as a support staff professional at an insurance company. In her first appraisal, Anne was upset at the bluntness of her boss's appraisal of her written communication skills. This year, she's determined to be better prepared to deal with his critique.

Which are the best examples of Anne looking forward to receiving constructive criticism during her performance appraisal?

Options:

1. Anne prepares herself emotionally to listen to her boss's criticism

2. Anne prepares how she'll respond positively to criticism she may receive during her appraisal

3. Anne prepares some suggestions for training options she'd like to pursue to improve her communication skills

4. Anne brings copies of her correspondence to demonstrate how her written skills have improved

5. Anne prepares what she'll say to her boss if he asks about her career goals for the future

Answer

Option 1: This is a correct option. Resolving to remain calm and professional while listening to what her boss has to say will help Anne demonstrate that she has a responsive attitude.

Option 2: This is a correct option. Being prepared to discuss the criticism will help Anne show her boss that she's serious about improving performance.

Option 3: This is a correct option. It's important for Anne to respond positively to criticism and be prepared to take advantage of the opportunity to improve her competencies.

Option 4: This is an incorrect option. Gathering evidence of accomplishments is important, but it isn't part of preparing yourself emotionally to receive constructive criticism.

Option 5: This is an incorrect option. Preparing what to say about your career goals is helpful, but it isn't part of looking forward to constructive criticism.

SECTION 2 - MAKING THE MOST OF YOUR ANNUAL PERFORMANCE APPRAISAL

SECTION 2 - Making the Most of Your Annual Performance Appraisal

The main part of your performance appraisal is a discussion of your performance. This is when you'll present your accomplishments. Be clear and confident, keep to the point, and recognize the contribution of others.

Your appraisal meeting is also a time for seeking corrective input. Acknowledge the validity of the feedback, remain calm and nonretaliatory, ask for clarification of vague comments, and work with your employer to establish an improvement plan.

RECOGNIZING STRATEGIES

Recognizing strategies

Your annual performance appraisal day is approaching. You've finished the first stage – preparation. This involved gathering evidence of your accomplishments, planning what you'll say about key issues, and preparing yourself emotionally for criticism. Now that you've laid that foundation, it's the time to think about the next stage – presentation. This involves how to conduct yourself during the actual appraisal meeting.

Performance appraisals are important to your career, so you'll need to be alert to strategies for achieving control and clarity in the actual process.

Although your employer will be the one steering the meeting, you're also a partner in implementing a successful appraisal.

You'll need to accomplish two main objectives during your performance appraisal meeting:
- present your accomplishments, and
- seek specific corrective action.

PRESENTING ACCOMPLISHMENTS

Presenting accomplishments

The first key objective is to present your accomplishments to your employer.

When you prepared for your performance appraisal, you should have gathered evidence of the key achievements you want to highlight during the meeting.

Your focus now is on how to present that information to your best advantage. Think about how you'll be perceived when you present your accomplishments to your employer at your appraisal.

Be clear and confident

Make your points clearly and confidently. Be careful not to sound arrogant or "full of yourself." Try not to appear nervous, flustered, or defensive. Use numbers and dates to specify how your achievements relate to your job.

Keep to the point

You're only going to have a limited amount of time, so it's critical to stay on topic – presenting your accomplishments. Don't waste time rehashing old grievances, or discussing irrelevant or redundant issues.

Present the information you want known – your career ambitions, for example. Don't get distracted, and if your employer veers off topic, gently steer back to the point.

Recognize others

Have you ever watched an awards show on television? It's rare that winners don't spend time thanking their employers and colleagues. They know it's important to a career to give credit where it's due. Recognizing others shows you're a team player and demonstrates your leadership potential.

Mika is having a performance appraisal at the company where she's employed as a junior manager. Follow along with each of Mika's statements for an analysis of how she presents her accomplishments.

Mika: These letters from our clients show how pleased they were with the rebranding campaign. I enjoyed being the team leader on the project and look forward to doing it again.

Narrator: Mika is clear and confident when she presents evidence of her accomplishments to her employer and states her goal of leading another project.

Mika: I'm pleased to say that the rebranding project was finished on time and under budget.

Narrator: Mika keeps to the point when presenting her accomplishments with the rebranding project. She is specific about how she met her goal and doesn't exaggerate her accomplishments.

Mika: Max was invaluable with the design and Lee negotiated a great deal for buying air time. In fact, our team worked very hard to make sure the clients' requirements were met.

Narrator: When Mika acknowledges her team, it shows she recognizes other people's accomplishments. This demonstrates both her empathy and leadership potential.

You've finished your performance appraisal with Antoinette. If you were clear and confident, kept to the point, and recognized the contribution of others, then you can consider this a successful performance appraisal.

Question

You work for a construction and renovation company. During the past year, you've worked on several projects, including your first as project manager.

Which statements are the best examples of presenting your accomplishments during your annual performance appraisal?

Options:

1. "I have the balance sheet from the restaurant project I led, which shows we came in right on budget."

2. "We met the clients' specifications on each of the five projects I worked on during the last year."

3. "My colleague Barrett was a great help liaising with the clients on the restaurant project."

4. "Well, I helped out with the museum project, but Lee did most of the work."

5. "When we were working on the university project, an interesting thing happened to our team on the job site."

Answer

Option 1: This is a correct option. You're clear and confident in expressing your achievements and presenting evidence of your accomplishments.

Option 2: This is a correct option. When you state your specific achievement, you're making sure to keep to the point when presenting your accomplishments.

Option 3: This is a correct option. By acknowledging Barrett's contribution, you show you recognize other people's accomplishments as well as your own.

Option 4: This option is incorrect. Although it's important to acknowledge others, you shouldn't deny your own part in achieving success. In this case, you're neither clear nor confident when you present your accomplishments.

Option 5: This option is incorrect. It's good to show confidence, but you shouldn't wander off topic. Doing so wastes valuable time.

SEEKING CORRECTIVE INPUT

Seeking corrective input

Now that you've presented your accomplishments, the second key strategy in maximizing the effectiveness of your performance appraisal is to seek specific corrective action to improve your performance.

Your performance appraisal is about assessing your past and present performance, but it's also about determining your potential and your future worth to your organization.

Remember, accomplishing what your employer considers important is critical to your promotability. Think about your appraisal as an opportune time to gain insight into your perceived strengths and weaknesses at work.

Seeking corrective action can give you the opportunity to advance your career, it can provide a platform for you to address performance issues, and it can make you better at your job.

Causes of negative feedback at a performance appraisal

Negative feedback can happen for many reasons – a misunderstanding, a wrongdoing on your part, varying points of view about what's important, comparison to coworkers, or failure to meet performance standards. But no matter what the reason, the important thing is to use criticism to your advantage.

You can use strategies to seek corrective action and turn negative feedback to your advantage: acknowledge the validity of feedback

remain calm and nonretaliatory

ask for clarification of vague comments, and

work with your employer to establish an improvement plan

You may not agree with negative feedback, but it's important to accept that your employer has a valid reason for making that criticism.

Keep in mind that employers relate the truth as they perceive it. It's to your benefit to acknowledge the validity of feedback to discover how you can improve your performance in their eyes.

Criticism can hurt. But it's important to remain calm and nonretaliatory when you receive a poor appraisal. Showing you're accepting and interested in the criticism shows you're open to improvement.

Not all employers are master communicators. You'll want to make sure you understand what your employer means when giving you feedback. When you ask for clarification of vague comments, it helps to restate the criticism and then ask for clarification. For example, you might say "You noted that I wasn't good at time management. How so?"

Once you're clear on what needs to be improved, it's time to work with your employer to establish an improvement plan. It's important that you both agree on improvements that will have the greatest impact in terms of time, energy, and career advancement.

Your improvement plan is a specific course of action that lays out what you'll do, when, and how your improvements will be measured. This plan is what you'll use over the next appraisal period to improve your performance.

Mika is going through her performance appraisal meeting at the company where she works. Follow along with each of Mika's statements for an analysis of how she seeks corrective input during her appraisal.

Mika: You're right to bring up the issues that resulted from my missed deadline last month. Are there any procedural changes that might prevent this from happening again?

Narrator: Mika acknowledges the validity of her employer's concern when she discusses having missed a deadline. Asking for corrective input shows she has an interest in what her employer deems important.

Mika: You noted that Jonathan said we had lost a client and attributed it to my work. Do you have any suggestions for how that type of situation could be handled differently in the future?

Narrator: Mika remains calm and nonretaliatory when faced with her coworker's accusation. She avoids defensiveness by taking a problem-solving stance and focusing on future behavior.

Mika: Would you clarify what you mean when you say I could be better at dealing with clients?

Narrator: Mika asks her boss to clarify the vague comment that she should "be better" at dealing with clients. Specific input and examples will make sure she and her employer have a mutual understanding of what "better" means.

Mika: I've noted your key comments. I'd like it if we could incorporate them into an improvement plan for the next appraisal period.

Narrator: Mika demonstrated she was willing to work with her boss to establish an improvement plan. This shows she has the motivation to make continuous improvement and solidifies the commitment of both Mika and her employer to her career path.

Question

You have finished the first part of your performance appraisal at the construction company. Your employers have concluded their appraisal and asked you if there's anything further before wrapping up.

Which statements are the best examples of using strategies to seek specific corrective input?

Options:

1. "I understand your concern about how my team communicated with clients on the project I led."

2. "I can't recall submitting any invoices late, like you mentioned. Let's discuss submission procedures to make sure I follow the correct procedure in the future."

3. "You noted that I could be more forthcoming in meetings. Could you give me an example?"

4. "I'd like to discuss setting some goals and measures for improvement over the next year."

5. "No. Nothing else. Thanks for your input about my work performance."

6. "I'm not happy that someone said I was late submitting invoices. That was an accounting problem, not mine."

Answer

Option 1: This is a correct option. This statement acknowledges the validity of your employer's feedback.

Option 2: This is a correct option. This statement is an example of remaining calm and nonretaliatory in the face of criticism.

Option 3: This is a correct option. An important part of seeking corrective input is to ask for clarification of vague comments.

Option 4: This is a correct option. Corrective input is the basis for year-round improvement. It's vital to work with your employer to establish an improvement plan.

Option 5: This is an incorrect option. At this point, you should move on to the second part of your performance appraisal. It's important to take advantage of the opportunity to present your accomplishments and agree upon a plan for corrective action.

Option 6: This is an incorrect option. Whether or not you agree with negative feedback, you should remain calm and nonretaliatory. Your employer probably wouldn't have brought up this point if it wasn't considered valid.

SECTION 3 - USING THE PERIODIC APPRAISAL STRATEGY

SECTION 3 - Using the Periodic Appraisal Strategy

The periodic appraisal strategy is an efficient and effective way to turn performance review into an ongoing process and put your career on the fast track. It consists of twelve assessments – one annual appraisal, three quarterly appraisals, and eight monthly appraisals.

These annual, quarterly, and monthly reports will increase your promotability by regularly highlighting your achievements, pinpointing the skills you need to build, and helping you maintain a healthy relationship with your boss.

THE PERIODIC APPRAISAL STRATEGY

The periodic appraisal strategy

Your annual performance appraisal is over. That's a relief. Now you don't have to worry about it for another year. Right?

Question

How often do you think some level of performance appraisal should take place?

Options:
1. Once a year
2. Twice a year
3. Every month

Answer

Option 1: Stop and think a moment. Do you really want to wait another 12 months to find out how well you're doing your job?

Option 2: Fair. But you still might be missing out on opportunities to advance your career.

Option 3: Good. Although you don't want to spend more time appraising than actually doing your job, the more often you assess your performance, the better the chances you'll be able to take advantage of opportunities to improve and correct behavior. Monthly assessments provide a good balance.

You may sit down for a formal appraisal once a year, but in reality, you're always getting feedback on your job performance. When customers are pleased or unhappy, they're judging your competence. When colleagues support you or let you down, they're sending you a message. When your superiors acknowledge or ignore you, they're telling you how much you matter. You can use this feedback to continuously improve your performance.

Your annual performance appraisal should be only part of a performance appraisal system.

In fact, performance appraisal is most effective when it's part of an ongoing exchange of performance- related information between you and your employer.

Traditionally, performance appraisal was a once-a-year meeting where employees were told where their performance was inadequate and what their targets for improvement were. But modern organizations are encouraging the concept of periodic performance appraisal – a continuous process that enables both employers and staff to make improvements on an ongoing basis.

You've heard the expression "Out of sight, out of mind." The periodic performance appraisal strategy allows you to keep your performance and your career goals in your employer's line of sight. It creates awareness of your productivity, achievements, and promotability on a regular basis. Regular contact with your employer allows you to identify and correct performance issues as they come up, before your career path is adversely affected.

Your employer usually organizes and mandates your annual performance appraisal, and it's your employer's responsibility to schedule and carry it out.

However, carrying out a periodic appraisal strategy is the employee's initiative. You'll need to let your employer know what you're planning to do and solicit support.

Remember, this strategy is all about positive performance improvement. Your boss will feel connected to your strategy if you're clear about how supporting you links to organizational goals.

IMPLEMENTING PERIODIC APPRAISAL

Implementing periodic appraisal

Typically, a periodic appraisal strategy is a month-to-month cycle that contains your annual appraisal, three quarterly appraisals, and eight monthly appraisals. This makes a total of twelve monthly components that are all important for documenting how you contribute to the organization, and how you're progressing toward your goals.

Twelve important documents are produced in a periodic appraisal strategy.

Annual appraisal

Your annual appraisal takes place once a year. It's a formal meeting where your work performance is assessed and measured, and where your goals for the future are established. Your performance over the last year is summarized and rated according to predetermined performance standards.

Quarterly appraisal

Quarterly appraisals take place three times a year. These are informal opportunities to touch base with your employer in a face-to-face meeting to find out how you're progressing toward your goals and what changes still need to be made.

Monthly appraisal

Interim monthly reviews are written self-appraisals that take place in the remaining eight months of the year.

In February, Mika went through her annual performance appraisal at the marketing company where she works. Follow along as Mika discusses how she uses periodic performance appraisal as a continuous improvement strategy.

When I had my annual performance appraisal, my supervisor noted that two areas for improvement were my time management skills and my ability to communicate customer requirements to my team.

My approach to improving my performance and showing I'm worthy of promotion is to make performance appraisal an ongoing process. Each month is now a step toward my next annual appraisal.

Question

What makes an annual performance appraisal different from quarterly and monthly reviews?

Options:

1. At an annual appraisal, job performance is rated by your employer according to predetermined standards

2. An annual performance appraisal is the one important opportunity to advance your career

3. Annual appraisals are organized and mandated by your employer

4. Annual appraisals are informal appraisal sessions

Answer

Option 1: This option is correct. At an annual appraisal, your job performance is formally assessed. Quarterly reviews are informal meetings, and monthly reviews are self-assessments.

Option 2: This option is incorrect. Quarterly and monthly appraisals are also important to improve your performance and build a case for your promotability.

Option 3: This option is correct. Initiating and carrying out annual performance appraisals are the responsibility of employers.

Option 4: This option is incorrect. Annual appraisals are formal, documented assessments of performance by an employer.

Your boss isn't going to see, hear, or sense everything that you do at work. Your quarterly appraisals are informal opportunities to present evidence of your performance gains and of your eligibility for promotion. You should document these meetings with factual assessments of your progress over the previous three months. Create a one-page summary of the meeting, with copies to the boss and your appraisal file.

The quarterly review offers a number of benefits. When you keep your boss informed during your appraisals, you demonstrate dedication, good communication skills, and a willingness to improve.

When you approach your boss with new ideas, you demonstrate professionalism, enthusiasm, and ability.

And finally, if you can anticipate issues and work on solutions to solve them, your boss will regard you as a valuable resource.

In your quarterly meetings with your employer, you should discuss both what you've done over the past

quarter and what you need to succeed in the future. You can cover various topics:
- special achievements,
- your goals and the actions you've taken to achieve them,
- any special recognition given to you by clients, customers, or coworkers,
- training that you've taken or would like to take,
- your career aspirations,
- issues you foresee arising in the near future, and
- new projects or initiatives you'd like to work on.

Follow along as Mika discusses how she uses quarterly performance appraisals as part of a periodic appraisal strategy.

My quarterly appraisals take place three times a year, the first one three months after my annual appraisal. This is my chance to sit down with my boss and let him know how I'm doing.

I also make sure to get my boss's feedback on my progress, particularly toward improving my time management and communication skills. I really feel this feedback helps us bond.

After the meeting, I create a summary of what was discussed and share it with my boss.

Question

What makes quarterly appraisals different from annual or monthly appraisals?

Options:

1. Quarterly appraisals allow you to identify and correct performance issues as they arise

2. Quarterly appraisals are informal opportunities to meet with your employer

3. Quarterly appraisals don't involve meeting with your employer

4. Quarterly appraisals are formal assessments of your performance arranged by your employer

Answer

Option 1: This option is correct. Quarterly appraisals are opportunities to touch base with your employer to ensure you're headed in the right strategic direction.

Option 2: This option is correct. Quarterly appraisals are informal meetings. Annual appraisals are formal meetings, while monthly appraisals don't involve meetings at all.

Option 3: This option is incorrect. It's monthly appraisals that are self-assessments. Quarterly appraisals are informal opportunities to meet face-to-face with your employer.

Option 4: This option is incorrect. The annual performance appraisal is an employer's responsibility, but carrying out a quarterly appraisal is an employee initiative.

Your monthly appraisal is also an important part of your periodic appraisal strategy. Monthly appraisals are written self-appraisals – they don't involve meeting with your employer.

At the end of the month, you document your achievements by writing a work summary based on goals and objectives set during your annual and quarterly appraisals. For example, you might summarize new accomplishments, record progress toward your goals, and note any issues that have arisen or that you foresee.

These summaries can be forwarded to your employer monthly and also used to support your quarterly appraisal documents.

Albert is in charge of circulation for a large university library. His monthly appraisals are concise reports outlining his objectives, related activities, measure of achievement, and results. For example, one of his goals is to improve library users' success rate of locating and using books and materials. The connected activity is redesigning the inventory control system. Using units reshelved as a measure, Albert shows he has increased access to returned material by 20%.

Each month, Albert compiles a self-assessment of his goals and the related activities, measures, and results.

But he realizes that it's also important to note any issues that have arisen or that might arise. After studying library usage patterns, Albert realizes that the heavy use of the library during exam times could adversely affect patrons' success rate of locating and using books and materials.

To avoid the problem, Albert includes the issue in his monthly assessment and suggests that staff hours should be increased during periods of peak library use.

Follow along as Mika discusses how she uses monthly appraisals and sums up her periodic appraisal strategy.

I write short appraisals eight times a year, noting the work I've done, what I've accomplished, and how I'm progressing toward my goals. I also note any issues that may have arisen or that I anticipate arising.

In particular, I carefully document how I meet each of my deadlines. I also gather evidence of how customer requirements have been successfully implemented. I sum the information up in a short report and make sure my boss gets a copy.

My eight short appraisals, my three quarterly appraisals, and my annual appraisal all add up to an ongoing performance appraisal strategy that documents my achievements, notes the skills I need to improve, and helps me maintain a positive relationship with my employer.

Question

Denys works for a large financial services company. He would like to work as a senior investment consultant some day. At his yearly performance appraisal, Denys was told he had good communication skills, but he needs to work on technical areas such as asset management.

Which are the best examples of Denys implementing the periodic appraisal strategy appropriately?

Options:

1. Denys puts together a quarterly report outlining his achievements over three months. He meets with his boss to review the document and discuss other issues.

2. Denys writes a monthly self-appraisal of his progress toward his goals. He outlines the training course he's taking, how it's helped his asset management skills, and how his record has improved.

3. Denys takes notes when he makes progress toward his goals and then compiles them into one assessment report at the end of the year.

4. Denys compiles a report once a year, but meets with his boss quarterly to informally discuss career goals and work issues.

5. Denys meets with his supervisor each month to review his progress.

Answer

Option 1: This option is correct. Denys needs to check with his boss each quarter after the annual appraisal to find out how he's progressing and what changes he still needs to make.

Option 2: This option is correct. For his periodic appraisal strategy, Denys needs to write a mini appraisal each month, outlining his objectives, related activities, measure of achievement, and results.

Option 3: This option is incorrect. For his periodic appraisal strategy to be effective, Denys needs to do an appraisal of some sort each month.

Option 4: This option is incorrect. The periodic appraisal strategy also consists of annual, quarterly, and monthly reports.

Option 5: This option is incorrect. Denys should compile a report each month, but he only needs to meet with his supervisor quarterly.

REFERENCES

References
1. **Manage Your Career: How to Develop Your Career in the Right Direction** - 2006, A & C Black Publishers, A & C Black Publishers
2. **Managing Your Career For Dummies** - 2000, Max Messmer, John Wiley & Sons
3. **They Don't Teach Corporate in College: A Twenty-Something's Guide to the Business World** - 2009, Alexandra Levit, Career Press
4. **Hospitality Employee Management and Supervision** - 2007, Kerry L. Sommerville, John Wiley & Sons
5. **Getting Promoted: Real Strategies for Advancing Your Career** - 2009, Harry E. Chambers, Perseus Publishing
6. **The Power of a Positive Attitude: Discovering the Key to Success** - 2008, Roger Fritz, AMACOM, 0814410138
7. **The Team-Building Tool Kit: Tips and Tactics for Effective Workplace Teams,**

Managing Your Career

Second Edition - 2007, Deborah Mackin, AMACOM

GLOSSARY

Glossary
   A
   aggressive communication - Communication statements that impart negative judgments and blame. Usually confrontational and dominated by "you" statements. See also assertive communication.
   assertive communication - Communication statements with no outward signs of negativity. Typically "I" or "we" statements are used. See also aggressive communication.
   B
   bilingual - Able to communicate in two languages.
   burnout - Psychological exhaustion as the result of stress on the job for prolonged periods of time.
   C
   career development plan - A process of strategically planning a career. Career planning is ongoing and dynamic and is used to help manage a career.

career updating - The maintenance or developmental updating of skills and knowledge needed to stay up to date in a chosen field.

conflict - A state of disagreement or disharmony.

D

delegatee - A person who receives an assignment.

delegator - A person who assigns work to another person or group.

deliverable - Tangible output of a work or development process completed by a specified time.

E

emotional intelligence - The ability to handle emotions appropriately and work well with others.

empathy - The ability to understand another person's feelings.

F

formal appraisal - The process of evaluating the performance or aptitude of a person in a defined and predetermined setting.

H

hard skills - Skills that are technical in nature and involve defined processes to practice. Hard skills are defined by their process. See also soft skills.

HR Department - Human Resources Department or personnel office.

I

informal appraisal - The process of casually evaluating the performance or aptitude of an individual through passive observation, anecdotes, and the individual's self-evaluation.

IT Department - Information Technology Department; sometimes known as the Systems

Department or the Information Services Department (ISD); the department consisting of the people who work with computers.

L

lateral move - A job change that would be viewed as a sideways move on an organizational chart.

leadership - The process of inspiring individuals to work willingly and enthusiastically to reach organizational goals.

M

mitigate - 1. To make less severe. 2. To alleviate.

motivation - The necessary expenditure of effort required to accomplish desired results.

motivators - Aspects of a work situation that motivate employees by providing positive job satisfaction.

N

network - An organized collection of personal contacts.

O

organizational culture - A system of shared beliefs and values that influence the behavior of people within an organization.

P

performance - 1. The degree of accomplishment of given objectives measured against preset requirements and standards. 2. An informal measure of the quality of a specific action.

performance appraisal - A periodic and systematic review of an individual's work and achievements during a defined period of time using predefined performance measures. See performance measure.

performance measure - An assessment scale for assigning a value to an attribute by comparison to a criterion.

performance standard - Norm-based or criteria-based rating scale that defines good versus poor performance for a specific attribute.

personal development - The act, process, or result of promoting the growth of interpersonal and intrapersonal skills, traits, or qualities.

positive feedback - An evaluative response or assessment of a process or activity intended to improve the performance or esteem of an individual.

professionalism - The upholding and positive practice by individuals of the principles, standards, competencies, and conventions of their profession.

R

rapport - A relationship marked by harmony, conformity, accord, or affinity.

S

self-assessment - The act of examining one's own personality preferences or traits and professional qualities to establish a plan for development.

self-direction -The ability of an individual to understand specific tasks and rules of behavior and then set the process in place to complete the tasks or conform to the behavior.

soft skills - Nontechnical abilities, talents, and traits required to communicate and interact effectively, and to understand and adapt to the culture of the workplace. Soft skills are defined by their outcome. See also hard skills.

supportive listening - A type of listening in which a listener is fully engaged, giving full attention, being patient, and seeking understanding.

T

time management - The process of planning, recording, and quantifying time spent completing tasks.

W

work style - The personal set of traits, communication styles, behavioral tendencies, and characteristics an individual utilizes to do work.

www.ingramcontent.com/pod-product-compliance
Lightning Source LLC
Chambersburg PA
CBHW020918180526
45163CB00007B/2784